WHEN HEARTS CONJOIN

Kendra

Kendra Deene Herrin

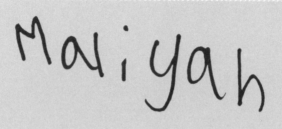

Maliyah Mae Herrin

WHEN HEARTS CONJOIN

ERIN MARIE HERRIN

with LU ANN BROBST STAHELI

RICHARD PAUL EVANS
PUBLISHING

When Hearts Conjoin
Erin Marie Herrin

Richard Paul Evans Publishing
65 E. Wadsworth Park Drive, Suite 110
Draper, Utah 84020
www.richardpaulevans.com

www.WhenHeartsConjoin.com
www.herrintwins.com

Book design: Fran Platt, Eden Design, Salt Lake City, Utah
Cover Photography: Adilfa Ford
Don Polo Photography, Salt Lake City, Utah
www.donpolo.com
Back cover photo: Brett Taylor

ISBN: 978-1-60645-036-9
10 9 8 7 6 5 4 3 2 1

First Printing

PRINTED IN THE UNITED STATES OF AMERICA

Dedications

———————— ℘ ————————

This book is dedicated to our five beautiful angels: Courtney, Kendra, Maliyah, Justin and Austin. You are each an important part in making this journey so successful. We know it hasn't been easy for any one of you, but know that we love you and will be a stronger family for all the sacrifices you each have made. Always remember who you are and what you stand for.

To my loving husband for being so supportive and loving me unconditionally and for believing in me.

To all of our family who supported us through all the good times and bad, and especially Grandma Patsy, who without all her countless hours of service this would have been much more stressful. And to Grandpa Lamar whose spirit and strength we felt throughout. And to my parents, Jeff and Janet Warren, who spent many hours at the hospital with the girls so we could spend more time with our other children.

— ERIN MARIE HERRIN

℘

My constant gratitude and continued love go to my five sons—Carl, Tommy, Chan, Kent, and Zachary—who don't always understand why Mom spends so much time on the computer, and to my husband Mike, who has always believed.

— LU ANN BROBST STAHELI

Acknowledgements

———— ❦ ————

Jake and our family would like to thank all the doctors, nurses, and hospital staff at Primary Children's Medical Center who helped care for Kendra and Maliyah.

To all the surgeons, doctors, and Operating Room staff that performed a miracle that day, we are eternally grateful for all your preparation, determination and the love you all have for our girls.

We want to give a special thanks to Dr. Rebecka Meyers, Dr. Michael Matlak, Dr. Peter Stevens, Dr. Alan Stotts, Dr. Faizi Siddiqi, Dr. Bradford Rockwell, Dr. Patrick Cartwright, Dr. Catherine deVries, Dr. Dan Evans, Dr. Simon Durcan, Dr. Joseph Sherbotie, Dr. John Sorensen, Dr. Edward Nelson, Dr. Eric Scaife, Dr. Sean Esplin, Bonnie Midget, Katy Stevens and Holly Moss-Rosen.

—Erin Marie Herrin

I'd like to thank Erin and Jake Herrin for allowing me to be a part of this journey through their family history and a special thanks to Richard Paul Evans and Karen Christoffersen for believing in my ability. A huge 'thank you' goes to my editor, Heather (H.B.) Moore, for bringing my name to the table to write this book and for the support she and the rest of my writer's critique group give me every week. Annette Lyon, J. Scott Savage, Michele Paige Homes, and Robison Wells—where would I be without you?

—Lu Ann Brobst Staheli

Faith makes things possible, not easy.

- UNKNOWN -

Foreword

In 2006, the world stopped to watch as the media reported on the events taking place in Salt Lake City, Utah. Four-year-old conjoined twins, Kendra and Maliyah Herrin, underwent a twenty-five hour surgery to separate their shared lower bodies.

The media reported hourly on the details released by the family, but the story did not begin in 2006, nor would it end shortly thereafter.

Even amid today's high tech hospitals and procedures, the birth of conjoined twins is highly risky and against most doctors' recommendations. The successful separation of conjoined twins can only be called a miracle. But all miracles have a story. And that story begins with the children's mother.

When I met Erin Herrin in 2008, I was struck by the strength of her love and devotion to her children. I, like everyone else, had read about her remarkable story in the newspapers and magazines, yet hearing Erin's story firsthand, I realized that there was so much more. While I had focused on the twin's challenges, I had never considered the real underlying story, the power of motherhood. I felt humbled as I reflected on the sheer magnitude of what a mother's love can accomplish.

The path was never easy for Erin. From the very beginning, when she chose life for her daughters (over several doctors' recommendations of aborting the twins), to putting her broken marriage back together, and donating her own kidney to her failing daughter, Erin Herrin's journey is one of sheer determination and the willingness to sacrifice nearly everything to keep her family together.

I knew this story needed to be shared with the world by Erin herself. We introduced Erin to Lu Ann Staheli, the talented writer we chose to help Erin write her story, and the magic began. In this book, *When Hearts Conjoin*, the real story is finally told.

I'm honored to introduce this amazing experience of sacrifice, faith and tender moments of quiet determination that can only come through the purest love. A mother's love. A mother's story. This is Erin Herrin's journey to claim her family and keep them close to her heart.

— RICHARD PAUL EVANS
#1 *NEW YORK TIMES* BESTSELLING AUTHOR

Chapter 1

August 2006

Some people believe angels are real. Some believe they walk among us. On August 7, 2006, on the fourth floor of Primary Children's Hospital, angels were there to comfort me on the scariest day of my life.

Jake and I, Jake's mom, and my parents were gathered in a large room and began our vigil as the team of doctors—six surgeons, two anesthesiologists, one radiologist, two urologists, and twenty-five to thirty support-staff—worked in shifts on Maliyah and Kendra, our conjoined daughters.

Jake's dad, Lamar, didn't live to see this day, but both Jake and I had a strong feeling he was an angel there with us, watching out for the girls. At a time like this, the line is thin between life and death. In addition to Lamar, other angels walked among us. The only time I'd ever felt so surrounded by guardian angels was in the celestial room of the Salt Lake City temple.

Today, their presence gave me a calm feeling that all would be well.

I was grateful for the assurance that our decision to separate Kendra and Maliyah had been right. For months now, medical experts had debated whether it was ethical for us to subject Maliyah to the additional risks the surgery would bring.

Would she be able to survive? I wanted to stay removed from the debate, but since the topic was about our children, and ultimately a choice Jake and I had to make, it was hard to close our hearts and minds completely to the experts' concerns. We wanted what was best for Kendra and for Maliyah. We wanted them to have the chance to live a normal life, and the doctors agreed—that came only with separation—the reason we were gathered at Primary Children's Hospital today.

Letting the girls enter the operating room this morning was almost more than I could bear. Only those who have given birth to conjoined twins can truly understand the agony that comes with making the decision and the pain that grips your heart when separation day finally arrives.

The national media delivered *Breaking News* reports of the progress of the surgery the entire day. People from our church brought food to the waiting room, though I had a hard time eating anything. Other family members and friends came and went—at one time thirty people waited with us.

Dr. Rebecka Meyers, who was the coordinating surgeon, and Dr. Michael Matlak, the pediatric surgeon, were in the operating room most of the time. They had given us a detailed outline of what stages the surgery would take throughout the expected twenty-four to thirty-six hour procedure. They promised we would be updated every hour about how things were progressing.

"Separating twins is never standard," Dr. Matlak warned us. "There's always a chance something will go wrong."

We didn't want to hear that, nor did we want to be alone. Our family had scheduled shifts to wait with us, always making sure that someone was home with the other three children.

And, of course, we had the angels.

⌇

About ten hours into the operation, the hourly report was late, and I started to panic. Why wasn't someone coming? Was something wrong? I'd had panic attacks before and I recognized the signs. I tried to breathe deeply to calm myself, but that didn't work. As a matter of fact, it got worse. I couldn't breathe at all. I started freaking out.

Jake's niece-in-law, Monica, and my friend, Mary, seemed to sense I was struggling and came to help me.

"Something . . . must be . . . wrong," I gasped. I didn't mean with me; I meant with Kendra and Maliyah.

"Put your head down, Erin," Monica said. "Try to relax." She stood behind me, lifting my hair away from the nape of my neck and fanning her hand to cool me off.

Mary offered a cup of water. "Sip this."

After a couple of minutes, my breathing became steady enough that Jake was able to give me a blessing. As an elder in our church, Jake held the priesthood authority to perform this ordinance. He and my father laid their hands on my head, and Jake offered a beautiful prayer, asking our Father in Heaven to renew my sense of peace as the surgery continued.

Once Jake was finished with the blessing, my racing heart slowed, and I started to sort through everything that was happening. The calm assurance I felt earlier returned.

Moments later, Dr. Meyers came to tell us they had made a discovery—the girls shared something more than everyone had originally thought. They shared more than their lower body, skin, pelvis, and the organs in that region.

The twins shared a pericardial sac.

Kendra and Maliyah were conjoined at the heart.

CHAPTER 2

❦

September 1997

I was raised in a very religious family with strict rules. We attend church on Sunday—every Sunday, for three hours. My parents' families were converts to the Church of Jesus Christ of Latter-day Saints. Great-Grandpa Cain had been baptized by the missionaries; Mom's dad joined when she was in high school. Membership in the church has always been important to me and to my family.

Jake's family was similar to mine. His dad was the bishop of their local ward when Jake was young and his oldest brother and a sister went on church missions. His mom has always been actively involved in her church work as well.

As Mormons, we believe sexual intimacy is to be saved for when you are married. I believed in that, but I was terribly boy crazy.

I was a junior in high school. My best friend, Brittany, and I liked to drive around town in her black Acura Integra with the music playing as loud as the stereo would go. We had a great time meeting new people, eating in local restaurants, and going on dates with different boys. My life was filled with good, clean fun, despite the fact we were both huge flirts.

Occasionally, we saw a black Honda CRX driving the same paths we took. Neither of us knew who owned the car, but we followed it for fun. We decided that whoever it was must have been older than we were because it looked so expensive. We couldn't have afforded anything like it.

One night as we were driving by the old skating rink, we saw the CRX again and this time our friend, Chevin, was in the passenger seat. He motioned for us to come the same way they were headed.

"Follow that car," I said, and we did, around the block and into the Godfather's Pizza parking lot. All four of us got out and Chevin introduced us to the driver.

"Hi, Jake," I said. I thought he was really cute, but he was just another boy in my boy-crazy summer.

We started talking, then everyone decided Chevin and I would switch cars for awhile. He would ride around with Brittany, and I would ride in the CRX with Jake. He was sort of cute and looked great in his sunglasses. Plus he had an expensive stereo system in his car that could make your hair stand up. I thought it would be okay to take a short ride with him.

We drove around for a little while and it's a good thing I wasn't shy, because Jake sure was. I didn't care. I could talk to anyone for hours, even though I was the only one talking. Eventually we returned to the pizza place to switch to our original cars and to exchange phone numbers. I really didn't think much about it at the time because I'd collected so many numbers in that last week. Like I said, I was a flirt.

So I said good-bye to my new friend, and Brittany and I were back on the road.

Several weeks later I was bored and started looking for all the numbers from the month before. I checked everywhere in my room and decided they were gone. Assuming my mom had thrown them away when she cleaned, I ran downstairs to ask where.

"They're in the kitchen trash," she said.

I went through the trash until I found the numbers. Jake's was on top, so I called him first. It was a pager number—those were the "cool" thing back then—I paged him and waited, and waited. There was no call back, so I paged him again.

An hour later, he finally called. We talked for several hours and I found out he was a senior at Bountiful High School, and that he planned to go to CCI for computer training until he was ready to leave for his church mission. My goal was to stay single until I got out of medical school. Jake laughed, but I knew it was what I wanted.

We set up a date for Friday night, deciding that a haunted house would be fun. I am a big wimp when it comes to anything scary, so when we got to the haunted house my hands were sweating. I think Jake loved having a girl hanging on him before we even got inside. He kept hugging and kissing me. I clung to him like a drowning man, trying to keep my eyes closed so nothing could jump out and get me.

Somehow he kept pulling away, forcing me to look at the monsters around me in an attempt to find him again. Despite my fear, we had a great time. If only he had known how really frightened I was, I don't think he would have teased me so much.

The next day I left to go with my cousin, Kirsten, to Blackfoot, Idaho, for a football game. I was sad to leave Jake because I really liked him and my mind stayed on him the whole time I was gone. I could hardly wait to see him again.

For the next year, we were together almost all the time, hanging out at our friends' houses. Eventually we started to steady date each other.

By 1998, we thought we were in love. Jake bought a sapphire promise

ring on our one year anniversary in September. He still planned for his mission and I prepared for college and medical school. But on Valentine's Day during my senior year, something happened that would change all of that.

We made love.

I should have been happy. But three weeks later, I wasn't feeling well—sick, tired, and I realized that I had missed my period. As I said before, our church teaches no sex before marriage, but we were two teenagers in love. We'd gone too far. I thought that I couldn't get pregnant. Jake knew he wouldn't be going on a mission.

It was my birthday, but instead of celebrating, Jake started asking questions about my illness. "Do you think that you have the flu?" He seemed worried.

"I don't think so," I said. "I'm not sick all the time, just at night or in the morning." I paused a second before adding, "I haven't had my period this month, either. I think I might be pregnant." Actually, I was fairly certain I was pregnant, but I didn't know how he would feel if I told him.

"My parents are gone," he said, "so you can take the test at my house. If it's negative, no one will ever know."

He seemed upset, but we went to the store and I bought the pregnancy test. We took it to his house and read the directions on the box. I peed on the stick and watched in horror as the first line came up. Then I held my breath as the second line showed—pregnant!

It was my eighteenth birthday—and I was pregnant! We both stared at the lines for awhile before either one of us said a word.

"What are we going to do?" Jake finally asked.

"How are we going to tell our parents?" I said.

"I'm more worried to tell yours than I am mine."

I knew exactly how he felt. I still had a month until I graduated. At least Jake was almost done with his schooling at CCI. We'd discussed getting married right after graduation. This meant we'd have to move the date a little closer.

"Guess we'd better settle on some rings, huh?" he said.

"Yeah," I said, but all I could concentrate on was the dread about having to tell my parents.

"Whenever you're ready, Erin." Our bishop's voice was calm, his face serene, as he sat across from me in my parents' home that Sunday afternoon.

His expression said everything I wasn't feeling. My emotions whirled inside me, the guilty voices crying in my brain, the tears coming from my reddened eyes. I couldn't make my voice work at all as I looked helplessly from him to Jake and back again. I was doing everything in my power to avoid eye contact with my parents who were sitting side-by-side on the faded couch. My older sister, Megan, sat in the wing-backed chair across the room, waiting.

The pause was deafening. At last the bishop tried again. "Erin, do you have something you want to tell your parents?"

I shook my head furiously. No! How could I possibly tell them what their perfect daughter had done? The eighteen-year-old daughter they didn't really know and her now not-so-perfect boyfriend. I glanced at Jake, hoping he would understand my message as I nudged him.

"No way, Erin," he whispered. "They're your parents, not mine." His words were not meant to sting. His parents already knew.

We had told the Herrins the day before. Welcome home from your cruise, and by the way, Erin's pregnant and we're getting married. His mother was crushed, her lifelong dream of sending Jake on a church mission gone.

A few tears later, both of Jake's parents hugged each of us and said, "Whatever we can do to help, just ask."

If only I trusted my parents to accept our news the same way. What were they going to say? What had I done? Surely they had guessed by now. They'd been through this before with another one of my sisters. That was part of the problem. They didn't want a second daughter to fall into the same trap, so they had become controlling, trying to keep me close to home under their strict watch. It hadn't worked.

Yet I hadn't planned to disappoint them, especially in this way. I was more frightened than I'd ever been in my life and no one seemed to be willing to come to my aid. Couldn't someone help me?

I offered my pleading eyes toward the bishop, but even he shook his head. Then he relented, just a little bit, and looked at my parents. "I'm here to support Erin."

I kept my face lowered but mumbled an unintelligible word or two.

"What did you say, honey?" Mom sounded like she was trying to stay calm, taking her cue from the bishop.

A fresh burst of sobs accompanied the tears that continued to pour from my eyes. Jake reached over and held my hand and the bishop let out a heavy sigh. Megan knew what I was going through. She knew how my parents had reacted to Heidi's announcement and tried to help me.

"Oh, for Heaven's sake," Megan finally said, "Erin is pregnant!"

I felt like I'd been slapped. My head jerked back in time to see Dad's pale face turn dark red. Mom's mouth pinched shut, forming a tiny pink line where her lipstick once had been.

"I knew something was going on," she said, each word clipped staccato. "You just didn't seem right."

"Erin and Jake are getting married," the bishop said, likely glad to finally progress the conversation. "They've decided on May fifteenth."

There certainly wasn't much more to say and my mother proved that as she remained silent for the next two weeks. I was in agony. It had been bad enough around our house when my sister had become pregnant before she was married, but my parents expected more from me. They thought I was the perfect child. My condition was the worst news ever, but I'd hoped they would at least be there for me.

Eventually Mom was.

Jake finished his courses and graduated and so did I. I could only hope that someday I would be able to attend college. Jake was dead-set against it. He wanted to buy a house, not pay for me to go to school. Maybe I should have realized then that our life together wouldn't be smooth—that we had different ideas, needs, and desires.

Somehow I felt like all of my plans were being put off to the side and the resentment started to grow. Didn't I deserve to get what I wanted as much as Jake did?

CHAPTER 3

May 1999

The wedding plans moved forward rapidly. While few people knew about the pregnancy, those who did were very supportive. Jake's cousin, who was a bishop, would perform the wedding. The ceremony would be in the cultural hall of the church a few blocks from my parents' house in Centerville. Jake's aunt made me a white dress with an empire

waist, hand-beading, and a long train—a reminder of the fairy tale wedding I had always dreamed about as a girl.

That morning, my mother, sisters, members of Jake's family, and our friends went to the church to decorate the gym, including the basketball backboards, with spring flowers and to set up chairs.

Nearly two hundred guests arrived to see me walk down the aisle on my dad's arm. I cried the entire way. Although I was happy, I was starting to wonder if Jake was really the man of my dreams. We'd made a mistake, broken the law of chastity, but I wanted the best thing for my baby, and my upbringing had taught me that this meant a family with two parents—a mom and a dad.

Jake looked like this was hard for him as well. That scared me and I thought *we can always get a divorce if this doesn't work out,* hoping to reassure myself that everything would be okay.

What a stupid thing to consider on my wedding day. I put the thought out of my mind and let myself enjoy the rest of the festivities, looking forward to the honeymoon and the start of our life together in our own little apartment.

Wedding and reception over, we headed off for our honeymoon in San Diego, California. We only had the weekend because Jake had a Monday morning interview in downtown Salt Lake, so it was two long drives and a short stay.

Of course, as newlyweds, and with a baby on the way, Jake needed a job, but he didn't get it. We didn't want to live with Jake's parents forever, although that is where we started out.

Eventually, he was hired as a computer networking specialist for the local branch of Smith Detroit Diesel. I got a job at Target where I stayed until I was eight months along and standing for an entire shift became too much for me. Then we moved into our own little apartment.

The last few weeks of the pregnancy, I prepared for the baby by taking childbirth classes, buying clothes and getting the nursery ready. That was easy because, since we lived in an apartment, we couldn't paint or anything.

༄༅

Courtney Reiley Herrin was born on October 29, 1999, at 1:28 p.m. after ten hours of labor and three hours of pushing. Almost immediately, she was rushed away.

"Is something wrong?" I asked. "Is something wrong with my baby?"

"She'll be fine," a nurse assured me. "This happens a lot. She has fluid in her lungs that needs to be suctioned."

The woman's words were not reassuring to a first-time mother like me, especially one as young and inexperienced as I was. I didn't relax until I saw my baby a few minutes later and she was handed over to Jake. He was going to be a wonderful dad, just like his own father had been for him.

Courtney was a beautiful baby—jet black hair and huge blue eyes—with a calm reassuring way about her. We could tell right away that she was taking in the world around her, ready to discover it all. She was a thinker and didn't cry much, but she had the biggest smile which she didn't mind sharing.

She was the love of my life and I knew I could never love anyone more than I loved her. I was in awe and watched her sleeping for hours at a time. Despite some early difficulty getting the hang of breast feeding, and a bout with postpartum depression that left me sleepless and not eating well, I overcame my concern that I was going to hurt my baby and learned to be a mom.

Jake had a great job that not only allowed me to stay home with the baby, but we could afford that first apartment in Taylorsville. We had settled into a routine and life was going great, although not always perfect.

Nothing is ever perfect.

First Jake's dad, Lamar, had Parkinson's disease and it was getting significantly worse. He was having increasing difficulty communicating, yet Jake's mom remained dedicated to his care.

Then my father's diagnosis of Stage IV throat cancer added stress to our fragile lives. He was given a zero to twenty-five percent chance of surviving five years and he had already beaten the odds at living so far into its advancement, the doctors said.

Despite the fact that Jake and I were still struggling, we prepared to go to the temple to be sealed as a family. The ordinance, which was meant to bind us together as a family for all eternity, was performed on June twenty-ninth in the Jordan River Temple. It was a tender ceremony, much more private and intimate than our wedding. Although

none of my brothers and sisters could attend, most of Jake's were there, including his parents. I had my aunts and uncles with me and my mom and dad.

Our sweet baby, Courtney, was brought in all dressed in white—a dress adorned with flowers that Grandma Patsy had made. She looked around, taking in everything, as though she already understood what it meant for us to be sealed.

I had strong feelings that day, knowing I would have Courtney for all eternity. But I also had the feeling from Jake that coming to the temple was too much for him and, in some ways, it might have been too much for me. I had mixed feelings about the two of us together. But we knew our parents really wanted us to be sealed and we'd felt the pressure from both sides.

Jake and I hadn't settled all of our differences. My resentment at not being able to go to college had started to grow, but he wouldn't listen to my reasons.

Instead, we decided to have another baby.

❧

On Courtney's first birthday, we told our family that we were expecting. But a visit to the obstetrician determined there was no heartbeat and a week later I was in same-day surgery for a D&C.

"It's probably a good thing, Erin," Heidi assured me. "You don't want to have a baby with problems."

"Yeah," I agreed, but in my heart I was still disappointed.

CHAPTER 4

September 2001

The marriage Jake and I worked on so hard began falling apart in our second year. I still wanted to go to college; he thought he had given up too much by marrying me.

"I don't know if we're right for each other," he told me one night. "We made a mistake by getting married."

I had wondered the same thing myself. There never seemed to be a resolution to our arguments and I wondered if I really loved him. Maybe we needed a break from each other. He suggested divorce several times, but I pleaded no. I begged for counseling instead, not wanting to upset Courtney's life, hoping to keep the happily-ever-after dream alive.

Jake didn't want a counselor at all. For months he stewed over leaving me. He told me that every time he thought of a good reason for staying, a list of negatives would overwhelm him. He didn't want a messy divorce. The constant barrage forced my own doubts to remain close to the surface.

"I'm not even sure I'm in love with you," he insisted. "Maybe we can remain friends, you know, for Courtney."

Friends? I didn't want to be friends. I'm ashamed to say I wasn't very nice to him. I yelled a lot and tried to convince him that he was just having a bad day, that he didn't really want a divorce. But I was wrong.

Did I love him, even if he didn't love me? Did I want a relationship? A husband? To be a family?

I wasn't sure what I wanted, but Jake knew what he wanted.

He wanted out.

I should have recognized the signs earlier. My body gave me plenty of warning. I told myself I had a late summer cold, maybe the flu, but the general malaise was more than that. A check of the calendar told me all I needed to know. My period was late, significantly late. More than a month late. Maybe two.

But being a working mom—at a day care—kept my mind too busy. I'd not been employed that long and I'd only found the job because I thought Courtney needed a friend. Quite frankly, I'd been bored at home all day long and it was nice to be around other adults. But since I'd started the job, I decided I didn't like having Courtney at the day care all that much—too many germs—so my mom sometimes watched her while I worked.

That wasn't true today. Courtney was with me and I had to work in case Jake really left and I needed a way to support myself and Courtney.

Jake and I had wanted other children before, but now?

Not knowing how I felt about the possibility, I left work at lunch and bought a pregnancy test at the grocery store. Once the kit was paid for, I hurried to the store's rest room, too anxious to wait until I got home.

Less than five minutes later, I knew the truth. Jake and I were having another baby.

Would this end the talk of a divorce? Would another child make our marriage stronger? The possibilities gave me hope our marriage could be repaired, our promises renewed.

I left the store but didn't return to work right away. I had to call Jake to tell him the news. I punched the auto-dial on my cell, nervous but excited. He hadn't said more than hello when I blurted, "Jake, I'm pregnant."

If only my enthusiasm had rubbed off on him. He was quiet, very quiet for too long. At last he said, "I have to get back to work." The phone went dead.

I returned to the day care, somehow making it through the rest of my shift. I'd been so desperate to have someone—anyone—share with me what I still viewed as good news that I told Courtney, "You're going to have a new brother or sister."

She didn't understand.

"I love you, Mommy," she said, giving me a hug before returning to her friends and the play I had interrupted.

What did I expect? After all, she was only two.

Determined to put on a good face, to be the dutiful wife, I prayed for the best and headed home when my shift was done.

We'd moved from our tiny apartment to a house in West Jordan, one we were buying. Tonight it was a good thing we'd moved. We had so much more room than the apartment had provided. The house gave us space to avoid each other. I fixed dinner, cleaned the kitchen, and put Courtney to bed, all while Jake sulked.

When I could stand the silence no more, I went into the living room where he flipped through the channels of the television. "Jake," I said, needing to know what he was thinking, despite his sour mood, "do you hope for a boy this time?"

Nothing about his demeanor changed. His eyes remained glassy, his tone flat. "Yes," he said.

I knew he was lying. He didn't hope for anything.

For the next few weeks, we danced around each other like water on a hot skillet. We didn't talk about the coming baby, we hardly talked about Courtney, and we didn't talk about our relationship at all.

We were like two strangers, moving in the same universe, but not the same planet. We didn't touch. We didn't talk. Nothing changed—until the evening after the twin towers of the World Trade Center came down.

It had been a horrific day. I watched the news reports, aghast at the number of lives that were lost, worried about additional attacks against our country—New York, Pennsylvania, Washington D.C. How was this possible in our safe little world? I didn't know that soon, Jake would drop a bomb of his own.

Courtney was in bed when Jake came home from the gym. I wanted to run to him, have him hold me and comfort me as I felt the pain of those who had lost loved ones. But as soon as he walked in the door, I sensed something was wrong. His words confirmed what I already knew. Something was horribly wrong.

"Come sit down at the table. I need to tell you something," he said.

I followed him into the kitchen, my heart pounding. He looked at me with those blue eyes that I loved. Then he looked away.

"I haven't been happy for a long time," he said. "I think we rushed into this marriage for the wrong reasons. I'm not in love with you and never have been. I've told you this before. I want a divorce." He took off his wedding ring and set it on the table.

I couldn't speak. I didn't know what to do. He'd never taken off his ring before.

Then he was gone.

I heard the television switch on in the next room and the repeated commentary of the day's tragedy. I couldn't make myself move. I sat, staring at the gold band on the table, all that was left of our marriage. This time I knew we were through.

I was only twenty and not ready to face life and tragedy alone.

When, at last, the daylight grew dim, I made my way upstairs to the bedroom—no longer *our* bedroom. I picked up the phone and dialed my parents' number, my breath coming in gasps. I had held my emotions in too long and I needed to talk to my mom or dad.

Where were they? Why didn't they answer the phone? By the time the answering machine picked up and I'd heard the message and beep, I was hysterical, letting all the hurt out at once.

"Mom!" I screamed into the handset. "Dad! Please help me."

But they weren't home, right when I needed them most.

I tried to call my brother and sisters. No answers there either. I couldn't stop the tears. I thought my life was over. I had failed as a wife and as a mother. My daughter was losing her father and I was losing my husband. I was frightened.

How would I ever make it through this pregnancy by myself? Where was my life going to go from here? I didn't have an education, no college degree. How could I ever afford to take care of these children?

No matter what, I knew I had to be strong. I couldn't understand how this had happened. Sure, we'd started off all wrong, but we'd put our lives together. We'd stayed together, been active in church, and even been sealed as a family in the temple. It was supposed to be for eternity.

After awhile, I was able to stop crying long enough to place another phone call. This time, the call was answered almost immediately.

"Bishop? Can I come over to meet with you?" His invitation to come to his office right away gave me a renewed hope.

By the time our meeting was over, my dad, Mom, and Megan had arrived at the church, ready to take me home with them, but I needed to go to my house so I could pack.

I spent the night there, but the next morning, I took the suitcases and Courtney to work with me. After work, I went to my parents' house to stay.

They had raised me to be independent, and I didn't like having to intrude, but it was safe, and Courtney needed a place to sleep. Spending time at home with Courtney cramped into my old bedroom with me wasn't easy. Somehow Jake's sister, Lori, must have realized that I needed to be in our house and Jake should be the one to move home.

She called to tell me he promised to be out by the next morning.

True to his word, when I arrived at the house, he was gone, leaving me to play the role of single mom. Only this time, there was the new baby to consider as well.

And the bills.

How was my seven-dollar-an-hour job going to keep us alive, let alone pay the bills associated with the house and the arrival of the baby? What if Jake refused to pay for anything?

The bishop made arrangements for me to get food and diapers from the church's storehouse, but there were other expenses. The house payment was due soon and I didn't have enough money to pay it. I couldn't ask my parents for financial help because Dad's medical bills for the cancer treatments were staggering.

Finally, I turned again to Lori. "Can you get Jake to help with the house payments?" I asked, despite my hesitancy to do so. I couldn't even talk to him, I was so upset.

She agreed, and the next day, I had a check for half the amount. A week later, he gave me the rest. With the mortgage paid, I once again called the bishop. He arranged for the church to give me the money to pay the utility bills and help with our other needs, if I was willing to come into the building each evening and clean up after the various groups who had used the facility that day. I was happy to do it and Courtney was a good helper. The job kept my mind off the separation and its repercussions.

But even so, there was something more that was causing me dis-tress—a nagging feeling had started deep inside me. Nothing was physi-cally wrong. Nothing that didn't scream, "You're pregnant." I was certain this pregnancy was different, that this time, I was having twins. Nothing indicated this was the case during my doctor's visit and the first ultra-sound didn't show it, but I was sure it was true. Panic set in and my heart raced to the point I thought I needed to go to the emergency room.

Am I having a heart attack?

The question alone was enough to assure me that I wasn't. Reassur-ance came over me and the panic attack subsided. Nothing was wrong with the baby, nothing that my being calm wouldn't cure.

A few deep breaths and I was fine. The baby was fine.

I suppose the knowledge should have been greeted with more en-thusiasm on my part, but how could I be happy? Jake and I were sepa-rated, he wanted a divorce, I had a toddler to care for, and I was four and a half months pregnant. The idea of one new baby under these cir-cumstances was overwhelming. The possibility of two or even three was beyond belief.

I wondered if I'd have to put the baby up for adoption. There was no way I could afford a baby on my own. I wanted my child to have both a mother and a father, something that didn't look possible right now.

But that wasn't all. I still had this sinking feeling that something more was wrong.

I tried to talk it over with my mom. She scoffed it off as indiges-tion. My sister-in-law, Amy, said I was crazy. I didn't tell anyone else. My friends at work were too harried with their own lives to bother.

I needed to find a way to calm the stress I was feeling. It wasn't good for me and it certainly wasn't good for the baby. I turned back to my roots, to the way I was raised, and spent as much time as I could read-ing my scriptures. I even set aside an evening each week to attend the temple, leaving Courtney with my parents or a neighbor for the couple of hours of quiet. I needed as much strength as I could muster and God was the only one I could rely on completely.

And He provided for me.

It was a good thing, too. A few days later Jake called.

"Erin?" Jake said. "I wanted to let you know that I've filed the paperwork for the divorce."

The blow hit me hard—we'd only been separated for two weeks—but I managed to speak. "But, I don't want a divorce. I'll contest it."

"Doesn't matter," he said. "I can get a divorce with or without your consent. I already checked with my lawyer."

I hung up the phone, devastated. Somehow I had hoped things could still work out. That Jake would be there with me for the birth of this baby. That he would have a change of heart, and that I wouldn't be alone with at least two children to care for and feed. I was sure this new pregnancy had sent him over the edge.

Even though I hadn't been sure before if I loved him, now that he was gone, I knew it without a doubt. I loved Jake and I wanted us to be a family for Courtney and this new baby. I began to cry, deep sobs wracking my body, making it hard for me to breathe. I tried to pray, but the tears were too great, and then my nose started to bleed. I felt out of control.

After several minutes, I slipped down to my knees and a warm feeling passed through my body. The bleeding stopped and my tears slowed, as I repeated the same words over and over. "Please, Father. Give me strength. Give me strength." My breathing returned to normal, as I added more words to my prayer. "Let me be happy and give me the strength to get through this. Help the two of us stay together, if it's Thy will." I stopped for a moment, receiving a strong prompting to pray instead for my unborn baby. "And, please, let my baby live. Let me be able to raise it, that everything will work out, and we will both be okay."

I was still afraid—afraid of being alone, afraid something was wrong with the baby, afraid I was having two. But now I felt some peace. I only wanted to be happy and the Lord knew best if that meant Jake and I were to be together. Despite the difficulties I had been facing the last few weeks, I was becoming strong. No matter what happened with my marriage, I would be strong. I sensed that something wasn't right about the baby, but I knew my concerns were now in the hands of the Lord and He wouldn't fail me.

But I had to do my part. I added a prayer of gratitude, thanking Him for listening to me and giving me comfort. There would be no more prayers for our marriage to be saved. Jake and I had to make our own decision about that, even though we needed to resolve some of our differences for the sake of our children.

I knew what I had to do next. I called my friend, Rhonda Goodell, and asked if I could drop off Courtney for a little while. I needed to go to the temple.

This became my weekly routine. The temple became my refuge and my strength, despite my previous worries. The house payment taken care of for October, I turned to my next problem. It was time to register the car. The tags were going to expire in a few days and I wondered how long I could manage to get away with driving it without being pulled over by the police.

Since Courtney was with Rhonda, and she had said for me to take my time, I decided to renew the car license. I thought I might have enough cash to cover the cost, unless the car didn't pass inspection and needed a repair. But I'd had the overwhelming feeling all afternoon that everything was going to be okay. That my trials were over.

Tell that to the auto shop.

"The exhaust levels are too high," the mechanic said. "You're gonna need a new muffler system."

"What will that cost?" I asked, knowing there was no way I could pay for it, not right now.

"I'd have to write up a complete estimate, but probably around five," he said.

"Hundred?" I knew the disappointment showed in my voice.

"Might be more," he said. "Depends on how far down the line we gotta replace."

"Thanks," I said. "I'll have to take care of that another time. What do I owe you today?"

He told me the price; I paid the bill then drove home, stopping at Rhonda's on the way so I could pick up my daughter. I was worried about how I would get the money for the repairs, but I knew the Lord has many ways to provide. One of them was for me to call Jake, even though I didn't really want to, but this call needed to come directly from me, not through his sister.

I got Courtney settled, then dialed his number. He answered the phone on the third ring, but I didn't give him a chance to talk.

"Jake? This is Erin. I took the car in to have it inspected and it didn't pass. It needs a new muffler and possibly an exhaust system. I don't have any money and it's going to cost around five hundred dollars. I need you to pay for it because I have to use the car to get to work."

I had said everything I needed to say. Now it was his turn. *Will he hang up on me? Will he refuse? Will he yell at me, saying he doesn't have any money to give me?*

"Okay, Erin. I'll put the money in your account."

I could hardly believe it. No complaint? No refusal?

"Other than the problem with the car, how are you doing?" Jake asked. His voice was soft, almost tender, like he really wanted to know.

We talked for about ten minutes—just chatting. When we couldn't think of anything more to talk about, we finally said our good-byes and I hung up the phone. What had happened? Less than a month before, Jake had called to tell me the divorce papers were filed, and now he was not only talking to me, but carrying on a conversation as though nothing had happened between us.

A tingle of excitement passed through me, leaving tiny goose bumps on my arms. For the first time in months, I felt happy. Jake and I were talking, like we used to, and I would have money to get the car fixed. Two things had suddenly gone right in my life, at least for the moment.

It had been such a good day that I didn't want it to end. After dinner, I changed Courtney and headed off to the church for an activity. The Ladies' Enrichment night was a great place to keep the evening from being quite so lonely and it put me at the church already for my clean-up job.

I could hardly wait for the socializing to be done after the lesson. The thought had come to me clearly that I needed to call Jake again. I couldn't imagine why or what we would talk about. We'd taken care of all the business stuff in our conversation earlier. Would he think I was trying to make him feel bad that I had been struggling while life was going along great for him?

Job done, back home, and Courtney down for the night, I picked up the phone and dialed. He answered immediately this time.

"Hi, Erin." He must have seen the name on the caller ID. "How are you?"

"Fine," I said. "I just got home from Enrichment. What are you doing?"

I couldn't believe my own tone of voice. Was I flirting with him? I decided he would think I had gone absolutely loony, but he started flirting right back.

"I'm at Kevin's house, but it's really boring over here without you."

"Sorry," I said. I couldn't help thinking that it wasn't my fault I wasn't there with him.

"Hey, can I come over and see Courtney tomorrow?" he asked.

"Sure," I said. He took her every weekend, but if he wanted to see her mid-week as well, I guess I didn't mind, especially since he was being so friendly. "See you tomorrow."

"Yeah. See ya," he said.

We had been apart for six weeks, but over the next few days Jake stopped at the house, called me on the phone, and even invited me out. On our very first date three years ago, we had gone to a haunted house and I was scared of the monsters. This time I was more scared about our getting back together than any ghouls and goblins.

Jake and I talked more in October than we had in the last six months. It might sound old-fashioned, but we were courting, seeing each other with fresh eyes like those days long before Courtney's birth and the problems that had driven a wedge between us—the immaturity and selfishness. Were we both realizing we couldn't live without each other? I wanted so badly for him to hold me and for us to be a couple, but I needed to know there was more love, more respect between us this time.

He asked about moving back home. Even though I wanted to say yes, I told him, "No. Not right now."

I was getting stronger, and our relationship was indeed getting better. The irony was the divorce papers arrived at the same time. It didn't matter. We could work it out. After all, we'd already made a lot of progress.

I tried to see myself growing old with Jake and I watched other couples, wondering if anything had ever come between them. There were so many unanswered questions for us both.

Yet, when it came to support, Jake was the one who was there for me, even though we were living apart.

CHAPTER 5

October 2001

Jake drove me to LDS hospital for an ultrasound late on Friday afternoon the second week of October. It was a beautiful day. The leaves were brilliant on the trees that lined the drive to the building. I tried to push away all the unanswered questions about our struggling relationship and marriage and enjoy the scenery.

The air was crisp, but pleasant, and I left the car window open to feel the breeze on my face. We had dropped Courtney off with his parents and, although Jake and I didn't talk much, it was nice riding with him. I could almost imagine it was like old times.

I was excited to find out if Courtney would have a brother or a sister. I liked the name Cameron Jacob for a boy, but neither Jake nor I had discussed the possibility of a girl.

The ultrasound procedure wouldn't be a problem—I'd had them before—but I still had that nagging feeling something was different about this pregnancy than when I'd carried Courtney. The thought that I might be having twins crossed my mind several times, even though the exam in the obstetrician's office hadn't indicated more than one baby.

I'd heard the heartbeat. It had been so strong, much stronger than I remembered Courtney's, and I had been surprised by how quickly the obstetrician found it. There was no reason to be concerned, so I tried not to worry. I didn't need to add anything more to my stress right now anyway.

Jake pulled the car into a parking stall, turned off the ignition, and said, "Wait right there." He jumped from the car, hurried around to my side and opened the door for me. He hadn't done that since before we were married.

I climbed out of the car and he touched my flat stomach. "Are you ready to get your picture taken, kid?"

The baby pushed against his hand. I could feel it. "Hey," Jake and I both said at once. Then I continued, "Looks like we've got a kicker in there somewhere."

"Football or soccer?" Jake asked, teasing me like he did when he was a kid—when we were both kids, just two short years ago.

"Does it really matter?" I asked.

The kicking had started in the past few days. Had it been this early with Courtney? I couldn't remember. And shouldn't I be putting on some weight? I was eighteen weeks along, after all.

"He'll be fine," Jake assured me.

It was nice to hear the words, even if my heart still didn't let me quite believe it. Jake took my hand in his and pulled me against him in a little squeeze. I had to look up to see his face, but I didn't mind. I'd missed having him around while we were separated, and it was looking like maybe he missed me.

"Should we grab some dinner once we're done here?" Jake asked, his voice sounding hopeful. I had made the appointment late in the day so he didn't have to miss work, but it would be evening by the time the ultrasound was over.

"Sure," I said.

After checking in at the main desk, we found seats in the waiting room, a place I'd always hated, but today I was really excited. Not only were we here to find out the sex of our new baby, but Jake had asked me out to dinner.

Things couldn't be looking better.

We found two seats together in a far corner and settled in, waiting for my turn.

Jake didn't like sitting in waiting rooms either, especially ones filled with expectant mothers, so he didn't have much to say. I spent my time wondering about the lives of these other women. Had their marriages been just as rocky as ours? Did they have regrets too? Would they give their husbands a second chance?

Only one other man sat waiting with his wife. He seemed nervous and I assumed this was their first child. Jake was so relaxed he was almost asleep, his legs protruding into the space between his chair and the row facing us. His eyelashes batted against his cheeks as he fought in vain to keep his eyelids open. I'd seen that peaceful look on his face so many times before, and I liked it. I wanted to enjoy every minute the two of us were together.

But as the time ticked away, the nagging feeling settled back into my gut. Then the baby kicked me, hard, on my left side. It had kicked Jake from my right side earlier. The word *twins* darted through my mind, but I tried to quash it. What if thinking the word made it true?

I glanced at Jake, knowing that our relationship had moved a tiny step away from that tenuous ground it had been on before. But we still weren't together, not in a real sense, and the thought of handling three kids alone terrified me.

"Erin Herrin?"

My heart leapt and Jake started. He rubbed his eyes then smiled. We stood and, once again, he tapped my stomach.

"Ready for your screen test, big guy?" He held my hand as we followed the nurse into the ultrasound room.

Soon we'd know.

Jake remembered the ultrasound routine from when I had one with Courtney. He helped me settle onto the tissue paper sheet covering the examination table. I pulled my shirt up to expose my belly. It was flat.

"I thought you said you were pregnant," he said. "Are you losing weight?

I was. Enough that I'd gone down two pant sizes. The stress I'd been feeling over our marriage and this pregnancy had been too much. I could hardly eat for worrying. I couldn't bring myself to say that to him though.

"Let's get this over with so I can go pee," I said instead.

"You said you want to go to the sea?" Jake said. "The river might make a better place to soak your feet. All this talk of water is making me thirsty."

"Stop it!" I tried hard to hold back a giggle. One glance at the sonographer had already told me she was all business. Jake must have figured the same thing out for himself, because he took a seat and closed his mouth, content to watch the monitor.

The technician squirted cold jelly onto my stomach and began exploring its surface with the ultrasound wand. The pressure against my skin made my heart beat faster—the thumps and gurgles through the monitor the only sounds in the room. In a few seconds, I would see the baby. Jake's eyes met mine and we smiled.

There it was. On the screen I saw the mini heart moving in rhythm, its own tiny swoosh and thump through the monitor. The technician held the instrument steady, pressing a little harder than was comfortable, but I didn't mind. A new tone joined the heartbeat chorus. The woman moved the transducer a little farther and a second spot beat on the screen, not far from the first.

"Jake, there're two!" I said, my hunch confirmed. "There are two heartbeats!"

He glanced at me, then back to the screen. "What? No there aren't . . ."

"She's right," the technician said. She moved the wand a little more, logging in a couple of measurements as she worked. "Two hearts and there are two heads. There's one." She moved the wand again. "And there's another one. Congratulations! You're having twins."

Twins. I had known it all along. I stared at the two round images and my mouth went dry. My eyes were glued to the screen as I was certain were Jake's.

I heard him whisper, "Twins." Then he was silent.

What was he thinking? Would our already fragile relationship crack completely under the strain of having twins? I'd seen other moms in the mall, or at the zoo, pushing those double strollers, tired looks on their faces. Would that be me? My emotions were on a roller coaster more dramatic than any I'd ridden before, but underneath it all was the fact I was having twins.

And I loved them already.

The technician moved the wand back and forth between each image. "It looks like we might be here awhile." She wiped the jelly off and sat back. "Why don't you go and use the bathroom? You're probably getting uncomfortable."

"A little." I wasn't sure why she needed more time, and they had never let me go to the bathroom during Courtney's ultrasound, but I did appreciate the break. After all, I'd had to drink nearly a gallon of water before the appointment.

When I came back, Jake took my hand. "I can't believe it," I said. "Twins."

He nodded, looking as shocked as I felt. "We'll need another crib."

I laughed, nervously. "Can you tell if they are boys or girls?"

"Not yet," the technician said before she motioned for me to get back on the table and turned on the machine again.

My heart soared at the thought of Courtney possibly having both a brother and sister. I had heard somewhere that was the most common combination when it came to twins.

"We're going to need a new car," I said.

"Maybe. Your car has three seats in the back," Jack said.

I laughed. "I think we need a van." It felt good to say 'we.'

Turning back toward the screen, I noticed the technician's lips were pursed. Now she worked in silence, her eyebrows scrunched close together. I watched her study the screen intently, her hand stopped mid-motion over the babies. I looked at Jake, and we exchanged questioning glances.

"Is something wrong?" I asked.

She started moving her left hand again, slowly, not making comments as she clicked on the keyboard, freezing images onto the screen then using the mouse to block off parts to study again. I could see the thumping pair of hearts, but that was all in the torso. "Do you see something wrong?" I asked again, hoping for an answer this time.

She made a grunting sound, continuing to work and stare at the screen. A pulse of dread shot through me. I understood she was one of those no-nonsense type people, but this was getting on my nerves. I'd never been ignored like this when I came in for Courtney. The technician then had been friendly, excited for me and for my new baby.

I didn't ask anything more, and Jake said nothing.

After a few minutes, she said, "Just a minute. I need to get the radiologist to take a look at this." She left the room without even looking at me.

I turned toward my husband, my eyes questioning, trying to comprehend if she saw something on the screen I didn't see. What's wrong?

Jake didn't seem too concerned.

Chapter 6

October 2001

W hat's that all about?" I asked. The screen was blank now. The wand lay on the table. I touched my stomach, making sure to avoid the area covered with jelly. Had the technician seen signs of Down's Syndrome or something? My younger brother had Down's so I knew how that diagnosis could affect a family.

Jake leaned back in his chair and said, "Probably nothing." But his face seemed to say something else. Was he worried, too? "They're making sure everything is okay . . . since there are two." The playfulness from a few minutes ago was gone. Had he noticed something he didn't want to tell me? Something I hadn't seen?

I tried smiling, but his return smile didn't quite reach his eyes. Something was wrong and I knew it. The minutes crept by, each one longer than the first. I didn't try to make small talk and Jake didn't say a word either. Five, maybe ten minutes passed. It felt much longer.

Finally, the technician came back, followed by the radiologist who took over the technician's place and started his own exploration of my stomach. He was an older man, experienced. *Good*, I thought.

Within a few seconds, he said, "I'm sorry to have to tell you this, but your twins are conjoined."

Something inside me froze. I'd heard the word conjoined before, but I didn't register exactly what he meant. Not what it meant for me. For my babies.

"I'm sorry," he said, his tone matter-of-fact. He looked at Jake, then back at me. "Your babies are conjoined. I can't really tell you much more than that. They are conjoined." As though he believed saying it again would give the word more meaning, the doctor repeated, "Conjoined."

Maybe the radiologist wasn't going to stop saying the word until I reacted. I started to cry. I wanted to get out of the room. Someone wiped the jelly off my stomach and pulled my shirt down.

In the back of my mind, I heard Jake ask about what organs the twins might share, and the radiologist said he wasn't sure. How was my husband remaining so calm? I suddenly wanted to scream, but no sound came from my mouth.

Somehow I sat up. Somehow I stood.

I watched the older man's lips move and I concentrated to listen.

"Take this card. It has the number of a perinatologist. We've already called for an appointment." He held the card out toward us.

Jake took it. I wondered if the man made carrying these cards a habit.

"What's a perinatologist?" I whispered, forcing the words from between my lips.

"An obstetrical sub-specialist for high-risk pregnancies," the radiologist said. "I'm sorry."

High-risk pregnancies? What about the babies? What about high-risk babies? And how many times was he going to say he was sorry, especially when he didn't sound like it? I didn't have a chance to find out. Jake led me from the room, his arm around my shoulders.

"What are we going to do?" I asked. "What went wrong? And what about our babies?"

His grip tightened around me as we left the examination room and moved into the waiting room. I sagged against him, not caring if everyone saw me crying. They couldn't understand my shock and confusion. The phone rang and the receptionist answered as if it were a perfectly normal day. I thought that the rest of the world should stop because my world had.

They say that life changes when you least expect it. And I certainly never expected this. Not after all that Jake and I had already been through.

My hope for a happily-ever-after white picket fence had shattered into a million pieces.

CHAPTER 7

October 2001

The first words out of Jake's mouth once we were back at the car were, "I guess I'd better move back home with you, Erin." But we had been down that road. I didn't want him to come back because I was pregnant or because the babies were conjoined. I wanted him home because he wanted to be with me.

Somewhere deep inside, I knew there was still pain over our separation beyond any grief about the twins. I didn't want to make another mistake. I surprised myself when I said, "No. Not now, Jake. Not like this." Where had I found the strength to turn him down? Hadn't I begged him not to divorce me? Didn't I need him home more than ever?

The look on his face told me he didn't understand.

"I need some time," I said. "And I think you do, too." I was terrified, but I knew it was the right thing for now.

I climbed into the car. Jake didn't hold the door open for me this time. He got in, started the engine, and drove toward his parents' house to pick up Courtney. He ran through a stop sign, proof to me that he was just as confused and worried as I was.

The silence between us was deafening, but inside my head I was screaming. So many things to think about—worry about. Where are they connected? Will they even live? I didn't know where to begin to sort through it all, but I knew I must. My eyes burned as tears built up again. I felt that as soon as we walked into his parents' house, everything would change. The last thing his family needed was one more health crisis on top of his dad's Parkinson's.

Had I done something wrong to make the babies conjoined?

Before I realized it, Jake had pulled into his parents' driveway. He let out a breath and I looked over at him. He met my gaze and I saw all my worries reflected in his eyes. Maybe this didn't have to be just my problem. Separated or not, maybe we would work through this together.

"We have to tell them," Jake said.

"I know, but what?" So far, we had no real information beyond that word—conjoined. We didn't even know if they were boys or girls—but this burden we carried was too much to bear by ourselves.

"We'll figure it out. Let's not panic," he said.

I got out of the car at the same time he did. Jake opened the door to the house and I stepped inside. It felt surreal. An hour ago we'd dropped off our spunky two-year-old, excited to find out whether we were having a boy or girl. That seemed so insignificant now.

"Mommy!" Courtney ran out of the kitchen and into my arms. I picked her up, burying my face in her shoulder-length hair, the shade much lighter now than when she had been born. I wanted to hold her for a moment, breathe in the child that I had created who was healthy and vibrant.

We found Patsy, Jake's mom, in the kitchen, doing dishes. She turned toward us. "You're back." I knew she could hardly wait to know everything by the tone of her voice. "Boy or girl?"

I couldn't get my voice to work. Jake said nothing either.

Patsy seemed to sense something was wrong. "Is everything okay with the baby?"

Jake and I locked eyes for a moment then he said, "Babies."

It took her only a second to realize what he meant. "Babies? You mean there are two?" Her dark eyes lit up with excitement, her round face, which was framed by short gray hair, wore a smile bigger than any I'd seen in my own mirror for weeks. "You're having twins?"

I nodded, feeling numb. Would she be so excited once she'd heard the whole story?

"Yes, Mom, but that's not all," Jake said. "Come sit down."

Her smile faltered, but she followed us into the great-room. Just then Jake's dad, Lamar, appeared at the doorway. I always caught my breath when I saw him. His frailty seemed to increase each day. His six-foot-one frame had shrunk over the past year and his natural thinness had turned gaunt. In recent months he'd been given a feeding tube and his slurred speech was almost impossible to understand. Lamar greeted us with a little wave.

Patsy helped her husband to a chair. I winced seeing him cling to her for support. How would he take our news? When we sat down I could hardly breathe, let alone talk. I knew once I opened my mouth, I'd start crying again. Somehow Jake had the strength that I didn't.

"Mom and Dad," he said, "the babies are conjoined."

I was watching Patsy, so when I saw her expression going from curiosity to shock to dismay, I couldn't help myself. I started crying. She brought a trembling hand to her mouth and her eyes filled with tears as well. I looked at Lamar. His blue eyes were watery—and although he might not be able to say as much, I knew he understood. Soon all of us—Patsy, Lamar, Jake, and I—were crying.

"We don't know the details yet," Jake said, hoping to reassure us all.

Patsy came over and hugged both Jake and me, catching our little girl in the middle.

Squirming between the three of us, Courtney asked, "Mommy, why are you crying?"

The group hug ended and I pulled Courtney tight into my arms again.

"Mommy's just sad," I told her. A tear formed in her eye and I wiped it away with my thumb. "Mommy is having two new babies and we are worried about them. But you don't need to worry, sweetheart. Everything will be okay."

Patsy asked, "What on earth does this mean for the babies?"

"We don't know," Jake said, his voice barely a whisper. It might just be some skin . . . but it could also be much more. We're going to a specialist on Monday to find out if they share organs."

His mom took deep a breath, perhaps steeling herself for the ordeal yet to come. "I have a book that talks about different things . . . like . . . like this."

She looked at me and I saw both worry and love in her eyes. I appreciated her concern and wondered how my own mom would react once we told her the news.

Jake stood. "Which book?"

"The book's cover is white. It's on the shelf in the other room."

He was back almost immediately. My stomach sank when I saw the title.

"This was the only white-covered book on the shelf, Mom. This can't be it," Jake said, as confused as I was.

His mother looked sheepish as she took the book from his hands, glanced at the table of contents, and turned to the page she wanted. She handed the book to Jake as I set Courtney down on the floor to play with a toy. Jake leafed through the pages.

"Mom," he said at last, "I don't think I can look at this."

I took the book from him, flipping the pages for myself, passing statistics like the tallest man in the world, and the shortest woman, finally arriving back at a section on conjoined twins. The passage below a picture of Chang and Eng Bunker, the conjoined twins who gave the condition the nickname Siamese twins, didn't say much.

I started to read aloud. "Monozygotic twins whose bodies are joined together during pregnancy where the single zygote of MZ twins fails to separate completely . . . this condition occurs in about one in fifty thousand human pregnancies."

How was my pregnancy the "lucky" one?

I had more questions than the book could answer.

"I'll take your father back to his room while you read," Patsy said. She helped Lamar from his chair and guided him toward the doorway as Jake and I moved to the computer room, Courtney in tow.

"See you later," Lamar said, although his words didn't sound anything like that.

Jake hurried over to give his dad a hug before he left the room. We probably wouldn't see him again for hours, maybe not the rest of the evening.

Another thought nagged at my heart; I had to tell my parents. But I couldn't. I'd caused them so much pain already and I couldn't spring another surprise on them, at least not without having some answers first.

Instead of returning to our house alone, I slept at Jake's parents' house, deciding it was better to put Courtney to bed there since she was already getting sleepy and it was so late. After her bath, I did her hair, then we read a book and said prayers. As I kissed her good night, my heart was heavy.

I slept in Jake's room. He stayed with me, trying to offer comfort. My tears wouldn't stop. I knew he was struggling too, but I was the one who wore the emotions where everyone could see. At least I didn't feel so alone with him holding me, and his parents in the house, but I still felt helpless.

"I think I need to move back into the house with you, Erin," he said.

I was too tired to argue, so I snuggled next to him and listened to his even breathing as he fell asleep. It was comforting to have him next to me again—it had been so long. But the old fears arose. Jake had hurt me so much and thinking about it now took my breath away. I didn't know if I could handle any more heartbreak.

At first I was confused about where I was the next morning when I woke up. Then I realized I was in Jake's room and the Herrin house. He was already gone from the room.

I had a dry taste in my mouth, so I stepped into the bathroom to get a drink. I went through the motions of getting ready for the day, using his toothbrush and comb, washing my face to erase yesterday's tears, and putting my jeans and shirt back on.

I went into the kitchen where Jake was eating breakfast. Patsy was there. Courtney must have still been sleeping.

"Can I get you something to eat, Erin?" Patsy asked.

"No," I said. "I'm not hungry." Actually, I couldn't imagine ever eating again. I dreaded calling my parents to deliver bad news, but I couldn't put it off much longer. "I wanted to let you know I was up. Can I use the phone?"

"Sure," Patsy said.

I went into the other room and tried calling the hospital to see if I could get any more information on the results. No luck. It was Saturday and I'd have to wait for my Monday appointment with the specialist.

Jake came in from the kitchen and sat down. I could tell that he was as worried as I was about this pregnancy; I just showed it more openly. For several minutes we both sat there, neither of us saying anything. At last, I dialed my parents' number, not sure exactly what I'd say, or how they would respond.

When Mom answered, I took a deep breath and asked her to get Dad on too. She didn't ask why.

When they were both on the phone, Mom asked, "What's wrong?"

"Well," I said, trying to keep the sudden burst of emotion from overwhelming me. "I have good news and bad news. The good news is that I'm having twins." I stopped, taking another deep breath.

"And the bad news?" Dad asked.

I couldn't answer at first. I gripped the phone, trying to control my tears which had already begun.

"What is it?" my dad's firm voice cut through my crying.

I felt like a child again, in trouble for something I had done. After a few minutes I was able to catch my breath. Squeezing my eyes shut, as if that would mask the reality, I said, "The babies are conjoined."

The other end of the phone went dead silent. Finally, Dad said, "What does that mean?"

"It means they are hooked together," I said.

"I know what conjoined means. What does it mean for the twins?" he said.

"We aren't sure which organs they share," I said. "We're meeting a specialist on Monday. A perinatologist."

"Do they have a chance for survival?" Mom asked, uncertainty evident in her voice. Leave it to both of them to cut to the chase.

I didn't want to say it, but I couldn't avoid the worst of the news. "What I read last night about conjoined twins says survival rates are not good. Sixty-percent of them are stillborn and another thirty-five percent only live one day."

"Oh, Erin." My mom started to cry.

I didn't know if she was crying for me or for my babies, but either way, it surprised me. "I may not even carry them full term," I said. "We have to go to the specialist and see what he says."

Both of my parents had questions, but I didn't have answers. We talked for a few more minutes. Mom reminded me to pray, but she didn't have to say it. I'd been praying non-stop since we heard the news. Actually, since Jake and I had separated.

Once I hung up the phone, a portion of the burden seemed to lift. At least my parents and in-laws knew. I felt like I'd jumped over a series of hurdles. I hoped I could hold it together until Monday.

Jake and I took Courtney back to our house mid-morning. I went straight to the computer and booted it up. While the pages were loading, I suddenly remembered something. I stood up and started to move toward our bedroom.

"What's wrong?" Jake asked, alarm in his voice.

I covered my mouth for a few seconds, disbelief pulsing through me. Then I told him the story that I'd forgotten until that very moment.

"When I was about sixteen, Dad and I watched a show about a set of conjoined twins. I still remember their names—Abby and Brittany Hensel. The parents talked about the struggle whether or not to separate them. They had to face the choice of sacrificing one twin to save the other."

Jake asked, "Did they separate them?"

"No," I said. "The girls did all kinds of things conjoined, like riding horses and playing volleyball. I thought that those two little girls were the most amazing people I'd ever seen. When the show was over, I asked Dad what he would do."

Jake remained quiet, but wrapped his arms around me, as he listened.

"He said he didn't know, but I remember saying, 'I hope I never have to make that decision!'" I wiped a tear from my eye. "And now, I do."

Jake pulled away and shook his head. "You don't know that yet, Erin."

I started crying again. How could we make the right choice? After a minute, I composed myself enough to add, "I still have the magazine."

"You kept it?" he whispered.

I nodded as a feeling of warmth passed over me. Maybe I had known someday I was going to experience this and needed their story to think about. Something that seemed insignificant so long ago now seemed extremely significant. Jake reached for me again, pulling me into his arms and kissing me. The atmosphere had changed.

Jake said, "Maybe their story will help us."

Yes, I fervently hoped.

"Why don't we search online?" he said, his calm logic taking over.

Courtney had followed us into the room, and I sat at the desk with my little girl on my lap and logged onto the computer. Jake sat next to me and put his hand on my knee. His gesture was reassuring.

I typed in the words: conjoined twins. The number of hits took my breath away. Over four hundred and fifty thousand entries on this one search alone. I didn't even know where to begin. As I clicked on a link, my heart pounded in my ears.

Next to me, Jake read aloud, "Births of conjoined twins, whose skin and internal organs are fused together, are rare. Their survival is anything but assured. Female siblings are three times more likely to be born alive than are males."

Suddenly, I wanted these babies to be girls. I realized I was holding my breath. The words wavered on the screen as my eyes filled with tears. Best case scenario, my babies had a twenty-five percent chance of survival if they were girls. My heart dropped. Would my babies be born alive? And if so, would they live more than a day? Would I watch them grow up? Go to preschool? Kindergarten? Would they ever be apart?

My heart was breaking and they weren't even born yet. Suddenly I wanted nothing more than to have these babies with me, to be able to raise them. I stopped for a minute and hugged Courtney, relishing the fact that I had her. She wriggled from my arms and moved over to Jake's lap.

I clicked on another page, a story about the Lincoln Twins in

Seattle—Charity and Kathleen—who were joined at the sternum and shared several internal organs. The girls had been separated successfully October 2, 2000, at the age of seven months.

Others weren't so lucky. As I clicked on more stories recounting separations, I learned that often one or both twins died during or shortly after the surgery. I stared at the computer screen, trying to imagine my babies in the faces of those other children pictured there. Did mine have a chance of being separated successfully, or would they even be born alive?

Every story I clicked on made me feel more hopeless. And helpless.

I had to find out as much as possible. Jake lifted Courtney into his arms and left the room, hoping to entertain her while leaving me to try to cope with our problem by doing research. I spent the next few hours on the Internet. Sometimes Jake stood over my shoulder, reading along with the tragic stories. I couldn't stop. The cold, hard facts screamed out at me.

One in one hundred thousand live births are conjoined twins.
Most die within forty-eight hours.
Thirty-five percent share a heart.
The prospect for long life is next to nothing.
Thirty-three percent share a liver or part of the digestive system.

I was desperate for answers from my own doctor. I wanted to know the type of conjoined twins my babies were and what organs they shared. At least I knew each baby had a heart. I had seen them in the ultrasound. At eighteen weeks, my babies both had beating hearts.

Beyond that, we just didn't know. According to the baby books, they should also have eyes, noses, mouths, arms, fingers and toes. Even that wasn't enough to ensure these babies would ever live apart, if they did live.

Instead of bringing home a new child—make that two—would I be planning a funeral? Would we need a casket instead of a crib? I didn't know how I would make it through the night without knowing, let alone until the appointment on Monday.

The more I read, the more I understood Jake and I would have to become the experts. We had to know what to expect—and what we wanted to do. We talked about what might happen after the babies were born, if they lived. There would be much to learn, but we couldn't imagine making any other choice than to have these babies and let the Lord decide.

In the meantime, Jake and I had Courtney to care for. We celebrated her birthday together and I made sure her costume was ready for Trick-or-Treating. She would be a monster, though only in costume. Just getting ready like this—and spending time together—made us feel like a real family again.

CHAPTER 8

October 2001

We arrived at the hospital, parked the car, and headed inside. Back
for round two with another ultrasound and meeting the perinatologist. This time was different. I hadn't needed to drink the gallon of
water before coming.

The room was smaller than last time, if that were possible. Maybe it
just seemed that way with the number of technicians, radiologists, and
specialists who were in and out, trying to unravel the mystery visible
only on the monitor.

Jake sat right next to me, holding my hand. His hands were as sweaty
as mine, so I knew he was also nervous. I was back on the table ready for
the examination, which would be lengthy. The same technician came
into the room. We greeted each other before she squirted the jelly and
began moving the wand across my stomach.

It took only a minute before I recognized the babies. I could see
their little round heads and, like before, their tiny hearts continued to

beat. But this time the sound was turned off. No accompanying swish, swish, swish like I'd heard Friday afternoon.

Actually, the entire room was quiet, voices kept to a murmur as the men and women, who knew so much more than I, pointed at places they wanted to view more closely. The images changed, the size of the babies increasing as the technician blocked off areas, then tapped the keyboard to enlarge the focus.

I strained to hear the whispers as they worked. I'd done enough reading over the weekend to understand at least some of the conversation.

"The brains appear to be developing properly. What do you think about their faces?" one doctor asked. "Does the structure look normal to you?"

Another doctor moved closer, peering into the monitor and running his index finger in an arc across a section of the screen.

My heart started to race. *Faces? Is something wrong with their faces?*

"They are very small. It's hard to see, but I think they're fine."

I knew the babies had to be tiny. I wasn't even in maternity clothes. The stress of the pending divorce and now this, meant I'd been throwing up for days. No baby-bump for me—twins or not.

"The heart chambers all appear to be intact," the first doctor said. "The torso is distorted, but the lungs are here. I can't locate a defined set of kidneys."

"Is this a leg?" the doctor asked.

"It could be." The man who said this traced a line in the air, following the tiny leg away from the body. "I don't see another one though. If only they were larger . . ."

"What about this?" the second doctor said, his finger now placed close to another faint line. "It's low enough on the body to also be a leg. The direction of the foot seems unusual, though."

Two legs. Only two? And something was wrong with one of them? That probably meant the babies were conjoined from at least the hips down. What else could it mean? I wanted to know more. *Do the babies have arms?*

I tried to absorb everything, but my mind was getting numb. What about their other organs? They needed them for their little bodies to function. I wanted these babies and I wanted them to live.

Nearly two hours passed before the specialists coming in and out of the examination room waned and the technician left, leaving Jake and me alone in the examination room with the doctor. I sat up and read-justed my clothes.

"The babies are so small," he began, "it's hard for us to tell much."

"We know they each have a heart and a brain," Jake said. "What else?"

I was expecting to hear about shared organs, so my mind almost didn't register the suggestion the doctor made next.

"You might want to consider terminating the pregnancy."

I could feel the color drain from my face. Jake's was already blanched. When had he come and taken hold of my hand? My mind was trying to sort through all the details, and the questions.

"They are so very small," the doctor continued. "They may not even make it through the delivery. Their chances of survival are slim."

"But they might survive," I managed to say, although my voice was nothing more than a whisper. "We saw their faces. They have heart-beats."

"I'm sorry, Erin," he said. "Survival is unlikely. And there is a huge risk to you. A modified Caesarean section, called a vertical section, would be necessary. You stand the chance of losing a great deal of blood. Giving birth to these twins might result in killing you."

He paused a minute, perhaps hoping I would accept his message. When he continued, I wanted to hear his next words even less than what he had already said.

"There are several ways to terminate the pregnancy. We can start you on medication—Pitocin—that will cause the uterus to contract so you'll deliver the fetus vaginally," he said. "But if that doesn't work, we would have to extract them . . . in smaller pieces."

Horrible images went through my mind. My babies being cut into pieces. *No! I refuse to kill them. These babies are alive!*

"What does that mean?" Jake asked, but the doctor moved to the next bit of information.

"Another method would be to inject a saline solution into the uterus which would dissolve the fetuses. You would give birth to the remains."

I thought I was going to be sick. I rushed toward the bathroom, hopefully before I threw up. I pushed the door shut behind me and kneeled at the toilet for several minutes.

Surprisingly, nothing happened. The feeling passed. I stayed in the bathroom for a long time, praying and crying. No matter what, I was having these babies. I got up and washed my hands and face, then headed to the examination room.

When I came back, Jake and the doctor were both seated. I could tell they had been talking. I had wondered for a second why Jake hadn't come to check on me, but I figured he had spent the time I was gone gathering more information from the doctor. I slipped into a chair and waited, feeling faint.

"Erin's health is the most important thing," Jake said. He squeezed my hand and looked hard at me. "The most important thing."

"I'll leave you two alone to discuss the options," the doctor said, then he left the room.

"I want these babies," I said.

"I know. I know," Jake said. "The doctor did make another suggestion."

"More gruesome ways to perform an abortion?" I couldn't fight the sarcasm in my voice.

"No, actually. He suggested an MRI and gave us a referral to see Dr. Rebecka Meyers." Jake put his arm across my shoulders. "He's made you an appointment for two weeks from now, Erin. I think we should come for the test before making our decision."

I breathed a sigh of relief.

Another test. Another chance.

"Thank you, Jake," I said. "Thank you for understanding."

I was going to give birth to these babies. But I wanted to go into it with as much information as possible. I'd continue to read and study between now and the next appointment and, of course, I'd pray. This wasn't a challenge I could take on alone.

But with both Jake and God on my side, I knew the babies and I could do anything.

Two weeks later, a Thursday evening found us once again sitting in a waiting room. This time we were at the University of Utah Hospital, basement level. It wasn't long before I was sent back into another area and given a hospital gown.

"Change into this, please," the technician said.

"How much do I need to take off?" I asked, hoping to keep something on. The room was chilly and my too thin body didn't keep me warm.

"Everything," she said. "Sorry."

Jake and I stepped into the cubicle and he pulled the flimsy curtain across the opening. Of course it didn't fill the space—the curtains never do. He stood in front of it, trying to help me maintain some sense of privacy as I peeled off my jeans, top, and underwear. I slipped my arms into the gown before he stepped behind me to tie the ribbons meant to keep the opening closed. The gown wasn't much more effective than the curtain had been at bridging the gap.

I reached an arm back to gather the material at my waist, hoping to at least improve my chances at keeping my bottom covered. Jake pulled the curtain along the rail again, opening the cubicle so the technician could see I was ready. *Am I ready, though?* I'd never had an MRI before.

I didn't even know exactly what an MRI was or how one was done. Oh, I'd heard the term on several medical dramas, but the patients on those shows were usually being rushed to or hurried from a test or operation and the technical side was lost on me.

"Erin?" The technician entered the room. "This way, please."

I followed her down the hallway, past a few more drawn curtains, a patient or two trying their best, just like I was, to keep their hospital gown closed and protect their dignity. Jake walked behind, making me feel a little more secure, but the act of walking was enough to push more cool air under my gown, causing me to shiver. Plus, the linoleum floor was freezing my bare feet.

"You okay, Erin?" Jake asked.

"Yeah, just a little cold," I lied.

In reality, it was much more than being chilly that made me shiver. I was scared, too. What would happen during the MRI? Was there something I was supposed to do? No one had given me instructions. No special orders before coming to the hospital this time, except I wasn't allowed to take any meds. Nothing. They listed several, including Valium. *Valium?*

"Nothing to calm your nerves," the secretary had said on the phone. My records listed that I was claustrophobic.

Of course, I couldn't take anything anyway because I was pregnant. Still, the doctors had to see the babies moving around during this test, and the meds that would help me get through the stress of facing the unknown would also calm the twins down, almost as though they were sleeping. I didn't want to take a chance at doing something that could bring them harm. Their lives were already too fragile.

"Do you have metal anywhere in your body?" the technician asked as we walked down the hall. She glanced at the clipboard she held in her hands. I saw my name at the top of the sheet indicating they were some of the forms Jake and I had filled out when we arrived. "Only a few fillings," I said.

She nodded then opened the door to the room where the MRI was to take place. "Here we go," she said. "The MRI provides detailed images of the body, better than a CT-scan or x-ray can possibly provide."

I tried to listen as I stepped into the room behind her and almost ran back out. Before me was a machine larger than any I had ever seen before. The thing looked like a fat donut with a bed that passed into the hole—a small hole. Why hadn't I looked this up on the Internet?

"Exactly how does this work?" I asked, wary of the answer the tech would give me.

"First you lie down on the bed," she said. "You're going in feet first, so it won't be as bad." Bad? Bad as what? "Once the machine starts, the bed will move you forward . . ."

"Into that hole?" I could feel the panic wash through my body and I hadn't even lain down yet. "No way!" I'd been afraid of small places for as long as I could remember and the opening looked like a soda straw in comparison to the rest of the machine.

"It's okay, Erin," Jake said, his voice soothing.

But it didn't matter. Threading a needle seemed easier than the possibility of getting my entire body through that tube was going to be. How could I ever make myself do this? I couldn't enter a tunnel barely big enough to clear my nose. Not for all the money in the world. Not for anything. Not even for the babies . . .

But that's exactly what I had to do . . . for the babies.

A female doctor came into the room. "Hello, Erin, Jake," she said. "Nice to meet you."

"Thanks," Jake said. I was too agitated to respond with more than a nod.

"Are we ready?" the doctor asked. "This test will let us see in more detail what's happening and how the babies are conjoined."

I guess she could tell that I was near panic. It wasn't because of what we might find out, but because I had to pass through that tiny hole and into that long tunnel. But the realization that I had to do this—*I had to do this for the babies*—brought my panic to an instant halt. There was no other choice. The MRI technology was the best way to see what was really happening inside my body, in my uterus, with my babies.

"Okay," I said. I took a deep breath, counting to five as I held it, then slowly let it out again. "I'll try. What do you need me to do?"

"Let me help you onto the bed," the technician said.

She held her hand out over the narrow tray as I lifted my left leg across and sat down. I set my right foot onto the bed and lay down, my head resting on the hard plastic surface. She helped place my other leg into position then lifted my left arm as I raised my right, tucking my hands together as though I was about to dive into a swimming pool. I could feel the panic building again. My head wasn't inside yet and I was already terrified.

"Hold still," the doctor said. "This won't take long."

"How is my entire body ever going to fit?" I asked.

"Good thing you've been losing weight, huh Erin?" Jake said.

I could tell he was trying to be funny. "Yeah. Good thing." But it wasn't a good thing. Losing weight when I should have been gaining wasn't a good thing. And neither was the noise that immediately started coming from the machine.

"Okay, we're ready," the technician said. "We need your husband to step outside for this one."

"No," I said, pleading in my voice.

"Sorry. Hospital rules," she said, but I wondered if it wasn't something else. Maybe they thought he was upsetting me too much.

When Jake was gone from the room, the clicks and whirs and grinding sounds on the motor seemed magnified. I'd never heard anything so loud before. I slapped my hands against my ears, hoping to stop the sound.

Suddenly, it was too much. We hadn't even started, yet I had to get out. There was no way I could go through with this. "Turn it off!" I said. "I can't do this. You have to get me off of this thing. Now!"

The doctor patted my hand briefly as I moved past her. "Hang on, Erin."

I could hear the technician. "You're doing fine, Erin. Just fine."

"I am NOT!" I yelled. "You have to turn it off."

"Erin." The doctor's voice this time. "You're doing okay."

I wasn't. I started to cry. "Get me out of here!" Only my ankles were in the tube. There was no way I could be all the way inside this tunnel without having a heart attack, if I wasn't already having one. My breathing became pants; a sharp pain pierced my chest. "You've got to stop!"

I heard the tone of the machine change. The bed was moving back the other way. I was being set free, but it wasn't fast enough. My heart palpitations were as rapid as those of a tiny bird.

When I finally emerged from the tunnel, Jake came back into the room. He was chuckling. Chuckling! How dare he? I sat up and looked where he was standing. Didn't he realize how scared I'd been? Didn't he know that small places terrified me?

I knew exactly when that realization struck him. The laughter stopped and his expression suddenly became serious.

"Oh, Erin," he said as he moved toward me. "I'm so sorry."

The technician hurried over to help me from the machine. "Would you like to sit in a chair for a minute? Can I get you anything? A glass of water?"

I nodded. The doctor stood on one side and the technician on the other. It was probably a good thing. My legs were shaking and my palms felt clammy. I might have fallen if they hadn't been there to support me. I took the offered hand anyway and moved to the more stable ground.

After a few minutes, I started to feel better, the panic having subsided. But I had to get back on that bed and get through this thing somehow. My babies depended on it. The doctor had realized I needed someone to talk me through this.

"Are you ready to try again?" she asked. "I'll help you."

"Okay," I said.

"Are you sure?" Jake asked.

"No," I said.

I stood and he walked with me over to the bed. I lay down, getting into the same position as before. The technician made sure I was centered and that my arms and legs were in a position to clear the tunnel walls.

"Close your eyes this time, Erin," the doctor suggested. She laid a hand towel across my face, blocking the bright lights from my vision. "Have you ever been to a spa?"

"No," I answered.

"Then you've missed a great bit of heaven on earth." She continued to talk, her voice lulling me into a calm state.

I flinched when the machine's ticking sounds began again, but the doctor didn't stop her story, the words coming into my ears in stereo as I passed into the tunnel where I could hear the little speaker above my head. She told me about places she had been, spa treatments she'd enjoyed, and the great massages she'd had.

The vibration of the motor shook the walls around me, but I fought hard to concentrate on the steady sound of the doctor's voice. I couldn't distinguish all of the words. The even tones and soothing way she spoke sounded like those meditation tapes. I felt like I was battling the giants, but I had to be strong.

Shortly, the scan was over. The bed had returned to its original spot, and I was able to sit up. I had made it through the hardest thing, despite my panic. The *first* hard thing. I knew more would be coming, but suddenly I somehow felt ready.

"Go ahead and change," the doctor said. "Then I'll discuss the results with you."

A few minutes later, we were back in an office with the doctor. The computer screen showed the MRI scans. I could see the babies. Jake and I sat down closer to the screen.

"This is the wall of the uterus," the doctor said, pointing to the lines that were shaped like a floating balloon, except there was no string to hold the air inside.

She zoomed in on the babies. Even my untrained eye could distinguish faces, arms, and hands, but nothing from that point down.

"Mush," she called the area beneath their arms.

My heart dropped. How dare she call my babies mush! I couldn't say anything though, I was so angry, and she continued.

"You can see right here where one baby ends and the other begins. Everything seems to be mixed together into one child from this point on. Just mush."

I wanted to stop her from using that word, but Jake could sense my frustration and held his hand out as if he wanted to stop me. "Are you sure?" he asked, sliding closer to the screen in an effort to see for himself.

"Yes," she said. She took a deep breath before she continued, her voice subdued. "I recommend that you terminate the pregnancy. You're a young woman. You can have other children."

"No!" I said, emphatically. There was no way I was going to kill these babies. Not now. Not after I'd seen their little faces on the MRI. They were too real. They might be connected to each other, but no more so than they were connected to me. The three of us were conjoined—in our hearts.

"Erin?" Jake said. "Maybe we should talk about this and let the doctor know our decision in the morning."

"No," I stated again. "Look, I know everyone wants what's best for me, that you're all trying to look out for me. But I am looking out for our babies."

Who else was willing to do that? As their mother, I was the one most qualified. Doctor's recommendation or not, I wanted these babies, and I was getting just mad enough to have them, no matter what anyone said. I knew they were special, even if they did only live for a short time.

These little ones were not mush. They were babies.

And I loved them.

CHAPTER 9

November 2001

Jake and I left the hospital not feeling any better about the pregnancy or the decision the doctors wanted us to make than we did when we walked in.

The two of us didn't talk on the way home. What could we say? This doctor had given us less hope and the MRI hadn't given us a clearer picture of the details when it came to the actual construction of the babies.

It didn't matter. I had already decided that I wasn't going to terminate and no one was going to change my mind. I hated the thought of an abortion even though my church gave them consideration if the life of the mother was endangered. I didn't think I qualified and I'd made the decision a long time ago, before Courtney was born, that my condition would have to be grave before I would ever consider aborting a child. I couldn't change my mind just like that because the babies would be born with a handicap. My brother, Josh, was born with Down's and he was my best friend.

Jake pulled the car up in front of our house and I got out. "I'll go next door to the Goffs' and pick up Courtney," I said. "I'll be right back."

On the way across the adjoining yards, I started to cry. I thought I was handling the disappointment and shock pretty well, but that obviously wasn't the case. I wiped my face and tried to pull myself back together before I knocked on the door.

Less than a minute later, Kirsten was there, a great big smile on her face. "How did it go?"

I looked down, not able to return her smile. "Not very well," I said. "They couldn't see anything more than before."

"I'm so sorry, Erin."

"Yeah. Me too," I said. "Is Courtney ready?"

"She's upstairs playing. I'll go get her."

She headed toward the stairs as I picked up Courtney's diaper bag that was sitting inside the front door. I heard my little girl before I saw her.

"Mommy!" she squealed and she started to work her way down the stairs toward me.

I opened my arms and, once she was close enough, I grabbed her into a big hug. We had become so close during the time we had spent alone together. No matter how hard the days had been since finding out about the new babies being conjoined, just being with Courtney made things better. I gave her a solid kiss on the cheek. "Mommy's so glad you're here. Ready to go home?"

She nodded her head. I put the strap of the diaper bag over my shoulder and thanked my neighbor for watching her.

"Anytime," she said as the door closed behind me.

Once home, I got Courtney into her pajamas and read her a bedtime story before looking for Jake. I hadn't seen or heard him since I came into the house, but that didn't mean he had gone anywhere. The car was still in the garage, and the house was big enough that we sometimes lost each other. I started my search on the main floor then moved to the basement where he often worked on projects.

Finally, I checked our bedroom. Even though Jake was living in the house again, I didn't really expect to find him there.

I opened the door and there he was, curled up in a ball, crying harder than I had ever seen him at any time. The stress was too much for him, just like it had been for me.

"Jake?" I moved toward him and sat gingerly on the edge of the bed. "Jake? Are you okay?"

He sat up and wiped his eyes before he spoke. "Erin, I want those babies, just as much as you do. I love them and they need us. Just like we need them. We can't terminate this pregnancy."

"I know," I said.

"We have to do everything in our power to help them get here safely and then we can take things from there," he said. "I can see myself raising these babies."

And I wanted nothing more than to have that chance, too.

He seemed confident with his decision. I had always been at peace with mine. I was so happy to hear again that he agreed with me. I was only twenty-two weeks along; so many things could happen between now and the time for delivery.

Now that I think about it, I'm surprised at how much peace I felt. I had been four when my brother Josh was born. Having a special needs sibling had not been easy for me, even though I loved him with all my heart. His Down's was severe and other kids treated him differently. People stared at us all the time.

I had looked forward to not having to deal with people and their prejudices any more once I was married and moved out from the daily interaction with Josh. As they say, be careful what you wish for. I was now moving toward becoming a mother to a pair of special needs children myself. I thought about my mother and all the things she had given up to care for Josh.

Then I thought about me. What would I need to give up for my babies? School would most likely always be out. Sure, living with Josh had made me strong, but would I be able to care for two children whose exact needs we didn't even know or understand yet? I certainly hoped so.

And as for Courtney, she was already strong. She was surrounded by family who loved her and who were willing to help care for her if Jake and I needed to concentrate on the babies. I knew Courtney would be the best big sister.

During the next few weeks, we tried to keep life as normal as possible, especially for Courtney's sake. I was twenty-four weeks along and doing as well as could be expected under the circumstances. I wasn't convinced I would carry the babies full term, or that they would live long after birth, but I couldn't bring myself to say that when people asked how I was doing.

On Friday nights, Jake and I bowled in a league with people from his work. Courtney loved going with us and playing the video games while we bowled. One evening, the adults were taking a break from the games long enough to eat dinner. Jake and I sat at a table with a couple of his friends when I saw Courtney go toward the ball rack.

"Jake, can you go get her?" I asked, concerned that she would get hurt near the lanes.

He stood and turned toward her, when just that fast, we heard a thunk and Courtney started to scream. The ball she had been holding rolled away from her as both of us rushed to see what had happened.

Jake reached her first, scooping her up in his arms. I arrived just as he discovered that her middle finger on her left hand was flattened, the skin on the back of her finger broken open from the force of the ball.

Her crying rang out across the bowling alley as I gathered our things. "We have to go to the hospital," I explained to our friends.

"There's one not too far from here," one of the men told us. He gave

Jake an address and directions while we moved toward the door.

As soon as we got outside, Courtney stopped crying, content to look around at the different scenery. She popped her finger into her mouth. *I love you so much*, I thought, and I meant it. I buckled her into her booster seat then got into the car myself.

Crying or not, Jake was frantic looking for the hospital. Although his friend had told him how to get there, the directions either didn't make sense, or Jake had missed something in his worry, and it took us several minutes to finally locate the building.

Jake dropped me off with Courtney at the Emergency entrance while he went to park the car. I hurried into the lobby and found the check-in desk. I showed the woman Courtney's finger, assuring her that the little girl's father was following right behind me to fill out the necessary paperwork. She took me at my word and escorted the two of us back so Courtney could be seen by someone.

I was positive the bone was broken, but I wasn't sure if it would need surgery. Jake had joined us by the time the verdict came down. It was broken but no surgery. Just a splint and pain meds and we could be on our way.

The doctor had also given us a prescription, knowing that Courtney would likely need more pain medication once this dose wore off. We left the hospital and headed for the pharmacy.

A few minutes later, Jake pulled into the parking lot and said, "I'll wait here with Courtney."

The lot was full, and I hoped these people were here for general shopping, not to pick up prescriptions. I dropped the prescription off at the window, then stepped away, hoping to find a place to sit down while I waited. No such luck.

I'd only been there a couple of minutes, when I felt an odd sensation. Suddenly a spot on my underwear felt wet. *Has my water broken?* I didn't think that was possible. I wasn't due yet for sixteen weeks, and Courtney had been only a week early. I couldn't leave without her meds, and I didn't want Jake to have to make a second trip. I thought I'd be okay. Surely the prescription I was waiting for would be ready soon.

Another spot, then I heard, "Courtney Herrin?"

"That's mine," I said, stepping up to the window to pay for the medicine. I grabbed the bag and hurried toward the car.

"I think my water broke," I said as soon as I got in. "I need to get to the bathroom."

Our house was down the street so Jake put the car in gear and headed there. He pulled into the driveway, and I got out of the car. I hurried in and headed for the bathroom, but what I found there wasn't the residue from my water breaking. It was blood, bright red blood that covered my underwear and had started to run down my legs.

"Jake," I yelled, hoping he had come into the house behind me. "I'm bleeding."

I heard the front door close, and Jake bounded down the stairs. He set Courtney on the floor outside of the bathroom then came in to check on me. "I think we're going back to the hospital," he said. "I'll call the Goffs to see if they can take care of Courtney."

He picked up our daughter and headed upstairs. I used a washcloth to clean myself up, rinsed my soiled underwear out in the sink then headed to the bedroom to change. I seemed to have stopped bleeding.

I heard the doorbell ring and Kirsten's husband's voice from downstairs as I finished dressing. "Take as much time as you need," he said. "Courtney will be fine."

"She broke her finger tonight," Jake was saying as I came up the stairs.

"Let me get her pain meds," I said, going toward the purse that I'd dropped on the floor in my rush to get to the bathroom. "She had a dose an hour ago."

"Don't worry, Erin," Paul said. "Kirsten and I will take care of everything. You need to get to the hospital yourself, so go."

Once in the car, I prayed for the babies to move so that I would know they were okay, and the Lord blessed me. About halfway to the hospital I felt a flutter, then a kick. *Thank you, Father. Thank you for protecting my girls.* I'd started to think of the babies that way because girls had the best chance of survival. I started to cry, but this time the tears were from joy. Courtney would have sisters.

Jake and I arrived at the hospital about forty-five minutes later. The Salt Lake traffic had been stalled, as is often the case on a Friday night. Of course, since we were in a hurry, our slow progress was more irritating than usual.

We parked the car in the tower and walked toward the entrance that led to Labor and Delivery. They admitted me right away and within only a few minutes, I had been checked out, the babies' heartbeats monitored, and we were declared safe to go home. I felt relief that everything was okay.

"It's sometimes normal for breakthrough bleeding to occur during a pregnancy," the on-call doctor said. "However, the spotting could be the first sign of an impending miscarriage. Nature does have a way of taking care of fetuses that won't survive outside the womb. When a woman miscarries, it is often because something is so wrong with the fetus that it wouldn't have lived beyond birth—if even that long."

I hated the way doctors were so clinical, so matter-of-fact. These were my children he was talking about, and I didn't want to hear about miscarriage and fetuses who can't survive. I wanted to say something to make him stop, but once again, I couldn't.

"Let's hope it's nothing to worry about this time," he said. "You're carrying conjoined twins, and they already have great odds against them. Just try to lie down and rest for awhile in case it happens again."

I took his words of hope seriously, but I didn't want to acknowledge the warnings. I was so grateful to have once again heard those two tiny heartbeats. Everything had to be okay even if the odds said they would not.

Once we were home and Courtney retrieved from the Goffs', I let Jake take care of her while I went to bed, propping my feet up and trying to relax. I slept fitfully, aware that Jake was up several times with our daughter, who was obviously in pain from the broken finger. Plus, she wanted her Mommy. I wanted her as well, but the doctor had said to rest if I wanted the bleeding to stop, so recovery was my main goal.

In the morning, I felt better. Having no blood spots was a good sign. I even had a little energy. That, too, was a good thing because there were lots of tasks I needed to do. I still had Courtney to take care of, I was terrified of spotting again, and, although Jake and I were back together, he had to go to work every day.

I knew I couldn't handle everything alone. One of my doctors had given me a card with a social worker's name and contact number. I was supposed to call her and explain about my pregnancy, and the needs I had for assistance.

When I got her on the phone, she told me she had never worked with the parents of conjoined twins before—actually, she was a student and hadn't worked with many parents at all—so she asked for a couple of weeks to find support resources for me. Since I'd been sent home from the hospital, I thought I had plenty of time before the babies would come.

We set up an appointment. She promised to find a support group and people who would be available to help us at home once the babies came. We didn't know what other needs would arise, but she was sure she could put together a resource file that would help us when the time came.

CHAPTER 10

January 2002

Two weeks later, I drove to the social worker's office for our meeting. She had stayed after hours to talk with me so that Jake could be home from work to take care of Courtney. Several of her co-workers were leaving as I arrived. All of them were interested to know about the pregnancy, and I filled them in a little before the woman and I slipped into her office to talk.

Although she had never had a case for conjoined twins before, the worker had been able to gather some basic information for things that I would need and services that were available to me. She would be at the hospital when I delivered, ready to help my family in any way she could. She tried to tell me what I could expect when the babies were born, but I had done enough research on my own already that she really didn't know much more than I did.

Probably two hours later, she and I had covered everything we could think of. I now had a page filled with contact names, organizations, and numbers for people I planned to start contacting the next day. There weren't many, and she said she had trouble finding resources, but I was excited to get going. I needed to at least try the numbers.

She walked me to the door, and I had put out my hand to push it open when I felt a big gush like I had started my period. "I think I'm bleeding again," I said, placing one hand against my abdomen and using the other to steady myself against the door jam.

"Do you need me to call an ambulance?" she asked.

"Let me go to the bathroom first to make sure."

She walked with me back into the building and to the rest room. I entered the stall to check. There was more blood than there had been before, and I felt light-headed. I sat for a minute, trying to keep myself from passing out.

"Are you okay, Erin?" she asked. She was in the waiting area by the sinks.

"I'd better get to the hospital," I said.

I pulled my pants up and exited the stall, heading for the sinks so I could wash my hands. They were covered with bright red blood. The social worker's eyes were wide as she watched me. I guessed she had never seen much blood in her life.

"I think I should drive you. We don't have time to wait for an ambulance."

"I can drive," I said. "I don't want to get blood all over your car."

"We'll be fine," she assured me. "I have a towel in the backseat. I'll fold it for you to sit on. Let's go."

Once settled in the car, I called Jake using her cell—the battery was dead on mine—and explained what was happening. He told me not to worry. He'd get someone to watch Courtney and meet me at the hospital.

Telling me not to worry was like telling me not to be Courtney's mother. Impossible! I tried to sense the babies' movement, but there was nothing. I prodded all the usual places, and yet I got no response. Of course, I started to pray. *Heavenly Father, please take care of my babies. Let them be okay.*

In a matter of minutes, the woman pulled up to the Emergency entrance at the University of Utah Hospital, helped me from the car, and we were down the hall toward Labor and Delivery once again. She had commandeered a wheelchair for me and kept up a steady stream of encouragement and support meant to calm my nerves.

What really helped the most was the movement I started to feel again in my abdomen. The babies were alive! I whispered a quick prayer of thanks as I tried to enjoy the ride.

CHAPTER 11

January 2002

Since I'd been here before, it only took a couple of minutes before I was checked in and taken to an examination room. The social worker stayed with me, chattering away about her classes, probably to keep her mind off what was happening to me. I had known she was young, but it seemed she wasn't any older than I was.

When the doctor came in, I gave him a brief run-down of what had happened, the similar event two weeks before, and the fact that my babies were conjoined. He immediately did an ultrasound, checking the babies' heartbeats. They were both there, so he skimmed over my chart, then said he wanted to go look at the computer records.

A few minutes later he was back, just as Jake arrived.

"I'll go wait outside," the social worker said. She slipped from the room.

"I think I'd like to keep you overnight, Erin," the doctor said. "We want to make sure this bleeding isn't something more troublesome than spotting."

Spotting? If he'd seen the blood all over me at the social worker's office bathroom, I don't think he would have used the word spotting.

"We want these babies to have a good chance for survival," he continued. "I'll send someone in to move you to a room." He shook both mine and Jake's hands, then he was gone.

"You doin' okay?" Jake asked.

"Yeah," I said. I really did feel better and lying down seemed more secure to me somehow than standing up. I guess I was afraid the force of gravity could make something break loose again in my uterus. If I had more bleeding, I worried that the babies might be forced to come too early. They needed at least six more weeks, but ten would be better. "Where's Courtney?" I wanted to change the subject. Maybe it would keep me from worrying.

"My mom came and picked me up. Courtney's with my cousin. Mom drove me here, then she was going to pick up Courtney and take her home with her until I get there." Jake continued to talk to me as the aide readied my bed and wheeled me down the hall toward a room. "I called your mother as well."

As though on cue, I saw her as we rounded the corner. She was waiting for me at the nurse's station."

"Hi, Mom," I said.

"Hi, honey. Are you doing okay?" She walked along beside us on the opposite side of the bed from Jake. "Is everything fine with the babies?"

"So far," I said, not knowing myself how long that might be true.

Once settled in my own room, nothing much seemed to be happening. I was getting tired. I knew Jake had to be as well. He'd been up since six, worked a full day, taken care of Courtney all evening then rushed here to be with me.

"Why don't you go on home, Jake? You can pick up Courtney so she can sleep in her own bed, and get some sleep yourself. I'll be fine here," I said.

"I'll stay with her," my mom said. "We'll let you know if anything more happens." My mom and Jake couldn't stay in the same room together for longer than a few minutes. There were too many angry feelings still between them, so I knew she would be relieved to have him go.

"Are you sure?" Jake asked.

"I promise. We'll call you," I said.

He came to the side of the bed and gave me a kiss before leaving, then I settled in to try and get some rest.

Shortly after midnight, I sat talking and laughing with my mother when a huge gush passed through my lower abdomen. I was sitting in a puddle the size of a life preserver. There was no way my bladder had held that much.

I pressed the call button.

"Is everything okay, Erin?" my mother asked just as the nurse answered, "Did you call?"

"Yes," I said. I had difficulty keeping my voice under control. I screamed the next words. "I think my water broke." Facts ran through my mind as I waited for her to either respond or come running. It was too early in the pregnancy to have these babies. They needed more time.

A group of people ran into my room, doctors, nurses, techs. They immediately hooked the monitors up to my belly so they could see what was happening with the babies.

"Everything will be fine," one of them assured me, but the way everyone moved told me they were as panicked as I suddenly felt.

The nurse came over to me, prepared with a pH strip, something like a litmus strip I had used in a high school science experiment.

"Here," she said. "Slide over a little bit. This will tell us if the fluid came from the amniotic sac." She dipped the slip of paper into the wet spot on the sheets. After a few seconds, she pulled the little paper back out to inspect it. "Blue. I'll call the doctor," she said before leaving the room.

Mom went into the bathroom, returning with a towel. "Let me help you clean up a little bit," she said. It was obvious she was looking for something to do.

It didn't matter. Before she could even get started, the tech was on the move. A portable ultrasound machine was wheeled into my room, the jelly squirted onto my abdomen, and the process was underway.

"You're in luck," the technician said after a minute. "There is still some fluid in the sac."

A minute later, the nurse came back in with a tray of medicines. "Antibiotics," she said, "and magnesium sulfate to stop the contractions. Doctor's orders. And you need more fluids." She noted the level of water left in my mug, jotting a note onto my chart before refilling it to the top and she hooked up a new bag to my IV before leaving the room.

The middle of the night or not, I picked up the phone and dialed home. I needed to tell Jake what was happening, like I had promised. He said he'd take Courtney to the neighbor's house and be up as soon as possible. I needed him, and I think he needed me just as much. Neither of us knew what was going to happen, and we were frightened.

Early the next morning, the doctor stopped in long enough to tell us that I'd be having another ultrasound. "Sometimes the sac can fill back up with water, and the hole can re-close. We want to see if that is happening."

I had a little prayer in my heart that it would. We needed more time if these babies were going to have a chance of survival.

"In any case," he continued, "I don't think you'll be going home anytime soon, as long as we can stall this birth from happening. Hope you're ready to be pampered for awhile."

Awhile was right. I had fourteen weeks until the babies were due, but they were planning to take the babies at thirty-six weeks, unless I

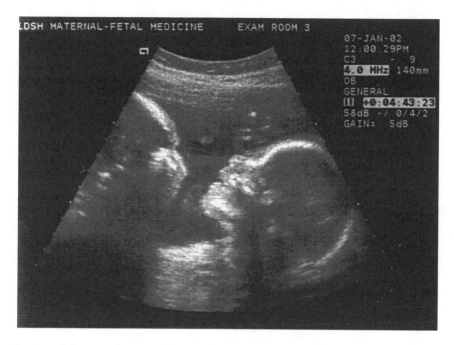

had to deliver right away because the sac didn't re-close.

An hour later, after another ultrasound, another prayer had been heard. The sac was filling back up with fluid and the babies were doing well. My gratitude was overwhelming.

About a week passed when the doctors told me that things were more stable with the babies. "I'm not going home, though," I said. I thought they should continue to be monitored closely.

Thankfully, the doctors agreed. My chart showed that just sitting up in bed or trying to go to the bathroom started another bout of bleeding. Sometimes it resulted in blood running down my legs or a pool where I was sitting. I couldn't take the chance of that happening when I was home alone with Courtney.

"The only way to ensure bed rest," Dr. Esplin said during his visit, "is to keep you in the hospital. Hope you're ready for the long haul."

I was. Every day we stayed under the watchful care of the nurses, the better chance these girls had of surviving. I knew it, and the doctors did, too.

But the twins had their own timetable in mind.

CHAPTER 12

January 2002

Every mother dreams of a having time to sit and do nothing. Spending ten weeks in a hospital bed isn't quite what that dream is made of. Of course, the real irony is that I was put in the hospital for bed rest, but rest is the last thing you really get in a hospital. Doctors, nurses, and technicians were in and out of my room at all hours of the day and night, checking monitors, asking questions, and wheeling me off for this test or that. It was all for the good of the babies though, so I couldn't complain too much.

My mom stayed with me as much as she could, and Jake was allowed to bring Courtney in to see me every other day. I could tell the stress of juggling his work, taking care of Courtney, doing the household chores, and coming to the hospital was wearing on Jake. And that meant it was affecting our relationship as well.

Once again we were struggling to get along, and sometimes it was over the most trivial things.

"Here's your laundry," Jake said one day as he dropped the suitcase on the floor near the tiny closet.

"Did you remember to bring the blue top I asked for?"

"Was it in the dirty stuff I took last time?" Jake asked.

His face showed he was tired, and I shouldn't have pressed, but I did anyway. "No, I didn't wear it last week. You took it home two weeks ago and didn't remember to bring it back then." I knew my voice was whiney.

"Then I guess it's at home somewhere," Jake said. "I can't do everything, Erin."

"And I can't do anything," I said. I tried to stop myself, but I couldn't seem to make my mouth just say 'thank you' and leave it at that. I hoped we could still sort things out once the pressure of living in two separate worlds had passed.

"I'm leaving," Jake said. He and Courtney had just arrived.

"No, I want to visit with Courtney," I said, still whining. My mom came into the room in time to hear me. She must have sensed what was going on.

"It's okay," Mom said. "I can bring Courtney home in a little while. Why don't you go ahead and try to get some rest."

There was that word again.

When Mom wasn't with me, and Jake was at work while Courtney was either at one of the neighbor's or with Grandma Patsy and Grandpa Lamar, I had a lot of time alone. I spent many hours reading from the Book of Mormon. It gave me the strength I needed to cope with the concerns I had about not only the babies I carried, but the family I already had at home.

I wrote about my feelings in a personal journal, and I also kept a journal for the girls about what was happening to them. The priesthood blessings my father gave me helped soften my heart and maintain my health.

Despite my fussing at him all the time, Jake did try to do little things to help me pass the time better. On Sunday evenings he would bring me some of the dinner his mom had made. He tried to sneak me out of the hospital to see downtown Salt Lake all decked out for the Olympics. Of course, I started having contractions and had to be hurried right back to bed.

And he was a super dad to Courtney. He told me about his efforts to potty train her—not quite as easy as learning how to do her hair. He had made arrangements for someone to watch her while he was working, and saw that all of her needs were met.

As hard as it had been for me when Jake left, I came to realize that it had been the best thing to help us both. The time apart gave us time to mature and grow. We became better people and better parents as a result.

Somehow we learned to appreciate each other more. Sure, we had our little squabbles—like over the laundry—but what couple doesn't? Once I realized that, I began to see the wisdom in Jake's leaving. The separation saved our marriage, giving us time alone to see what we really wanted and what we were missing by being apart.

Don't get me wrong—I wouldn't recommend separation for every couple, but in retrospect, it turned out to be the absolute best thing that could have happened for Jake and me. Despite all the suffering and heartache, I thank him all the time for leaving. It made us both stronger.

And being strong was exactly what we would need.

My obstetrician came in to check on me often, sometimes just sitting down to talk. He was worried about both me and the babies. He'd been doing a lot of research about conjoined twins, and he still didn't know if they would survive.

In my mind, I thought that my babies were going to die; everyone had said so. One of the techs who did the ultrasound had made me cry because she couldn't find the heartbeat. I thought they were already gone. I started to think about what I was going to bury them in.

I had hope, but I wasn't sure what would happen. I tried to keep up my own spirits. I wanted to feel like life was normal. Every night I showered, and the nurses said they could smell my Victoria's Secret lotion all the way down the hall. They teased me and said that they were jealous.

I had visitors, and of course I saw the doctors, nurses, and techs all the time, but I was still lonely. I yearned for the touch of someone who wasn't medical.

One night my sister, Megan, brought up dinner and gave me a card. I had a hard time holding back the tears as I recognized the opening words of my favorite poem.

> *One night a man had a dream.*
> *He dreamed he was walking along the beach with the Lord . . .*

Like the man in the poem, I, too, was at a time in my life when I needed to be carried, and the only one who could carry me, and my babies, was the Lord.

CHAPTER 13

February 2002

Afenter six weeks, I was ready for the babies to come anytime. I was so tired of daytime television and being in the hospital altogether. My parents and sisters visited, as did members of Jake's family. But for too many hours a day, I was alone in my room.

On February 26th—a Tuesday—I had been sitting up in the hospital bed, watching TV. At the commercial break, I decided to go to the bathroom.

I was back in bed less than two minutes later when I felt another gush. I looked between my legs to see blood and water spreading out across the white sheets. *Oh no*, I thought. I shifted my weight and realized there was another sensation—something I'd not felt before. It was as though something was coming out after the fluids. *My babies!*

I used the call button and waited, but nobody came. It felt like I needed to push for a delivery, and the fluids continued to drain from me. I hit the call button again, then glanced at the clock. It was time for the nursing staff's shift change. Would it take a miracle for someone to come help me? I had asked one of the nurses a few days ago what I should do if I was in trouble and needed help immediately.

"Pull the cord from the wall, and people will come running," she had told me.

So, that's exactly what I did, I grabbed the cord and pulled.

She'd been right. Immediately a nurse and two aides ran into my room and saw what was happening. They shoved the chair and tray table out of the way, closed the door into the hallway once the doctor arrived, and the nurse yanked the sheet away from my legs.

"I need to push," I said, the words nearly choking in my throat. I made myself remember to breathe in short little pants.

"Let's have a look," the doctor said. He had me lie back, bending my knees so he could get a closer look at what was happening near the area. He moved his hands against my inner thigh and touched the vulva. "I don't see any crowning. I think it's likely you've passed a blot clot and another one is forming at the vaginal opening. I don't want to take any chances though. Let's get her into delivery."

"What?" I couldn't believe the doctor was ready to take me so fast. I hadn't had contractions, and the babies didn't feel like they had dropped into place. "But they're only thirty-two weeks!"

"We can't take the chance of them trying to come naturally," he added. "You'd not be able to deliver them with the way they are joined together."

I knew this, but it still came as a shock that we were going into delivery now. "I need to call Jake," I managed.

"Of course," he said. "I'll see you in a few minutes."

The nurse handed me the phone, dialing the number as the door closed behind the retreating doctor. "Jake?" I said as he answered the phone. The nurse left, as well as one of the aides. The social worker stayed and another aide was prepping my IV and trying to clean me up a little before moving me to the operating room. "Jake, they're taking me into delivery."

"I'm on my way," he said then hung up the phone.

"I need to make one more call," I said and the aide came to help me dial. "Mom?" I said once the call was answered. "The babies are on their way."

I hung up and the aide returned the handset to its cradle. "Ready?" she asked.

"As ready as I'll ever be," I said.

I only hoped it wasn't a lie.

On February 26th, 2002, at 7:18 p.m., Kendra Deene and Maliyah Mae Herrin were born. I was fully awake, despite the C-section, although I did have an epidural to block the pain of the incision. Jake was at my side the whole time.

I couldn't sit up and because the babies were on a bed higher than mine, I couldn't lift myself up enough to see them. One of the girls cried before they were rushed away. A set of doctors and nurses cared for me; another group worked with the babies.

Jake came with me into the recovery room; the rest of our family was in the waiting room.

My first glimpse of the girls was a picture taken by the doctor so I could see what the babies looked like, and how they were conjoined. I first noticed how beautiful they were and how much jet black hair they had, just like Courtney had when she was born. I really didn't care what their bodies looked like; they were perfect in my eyes, no matter what.

I was assured the girls were doing okay, even though they were only six pounds four ounces together and too small to survive on their own. They had been taken to Newborn Intensive Care Unit (NICU).

"You'll be able to see them soon," the nurse told me.

Despite the reality of their bodies being fused into one from the chest down, the joy of relief passed through my heart. My little girls were doing well. Everything would work out, somehow.

I just needed to keep enough faith.

The staff continued to work with the girls, using all their skills and knowledge to stabilize the babies.

When the nurses brought the babies back into the recovery room, I sat up in bed, wanting to drink in every sound and smell, explore every inch of their little body. But there were so many people, and everyone else wanted to see for themselves how the girls were joined, trying to remove the blanket wrapped around them to keep the girls' privacy covered.

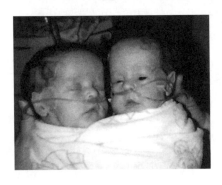

I didn't even get to hold them and could barely see them through the gathering of specialists, doctors, nurses, and technicians. I wanted to yell at everyone to get out of the room so I could see my babies. I wasn't sure how much time I would have with them. But I was able to keep my voice calm.

"Please, don't," I asked, wishing for these precious moments alone with my husband and daughters. "Please keep them covered."

My family and Grandma Patsy came into the room, and again I begged for the girls to be given their privacy.

The time with the girls was short because they were being taken to Primary Children's Medical Center where they would receive the best care of specialist physicians. PCMC was connected to the University Hospital by an elevated walkway, but to me it felt like they were going far away forever.

They were going to NICU, and I was going to hell.

Back in my room, I couldn't help but be relieved. My daughters had been born; they were alive; and all seemed to be going well. But here I

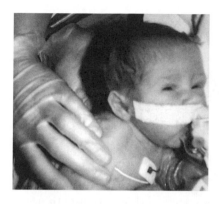 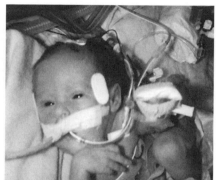

was, back in the prison I'd lived in for the past six weeks, my babies gone to another place, and suddenly I felt so alone. The emotions soon became overwhelming. As difficult as this pregnancy had been, I missed the presence of those babies inside me. Now I was empty, and even though I was rarely alone, I couldn't shake the feeling.

My mom stayed with me as I cried all night. I wanted so badly to hold my babies, to touch their tiny faces. I blamed myself for their early birth, and I prayed that all of the suffering they were going through right now could be taken away. If only it could happen to me not them. They were so tiny and my body had turned against them, forcing them into this world before their time.

"When will I get to go see them again?" I asked my mom. Of course, she didn't know. And I couldn't explain how I was feeling. I had moved into a dark place. Empty, yet awash with feeling. What had they given me during the C-section? I didn't know if that was the cause or if I had fallen back into the postpartum depression already like I'd suffered after Courtney's birth.

I passed the night crying, wishing I could see the babies. Finally, my wish was granted. At four-thirty, one of my aides, who'd become like a best friend, came into my room. She knew I was awake because I had called out every twenty minutes to see if I could see my babies yet. The doctors had encouraged me not to, but I was determined. The emptiness I felt inside was so overwhelming.

"What is it?" I asked when she just waited at the foot of my bed.

"Primary Children's is ready for you," she answered.

I slowly got out of bed with the help of the aide and my mom, and I sat in the wheelchair. It didn't matter to me that I had just had major surgery; I was going to see my little girls. I'd seen the pictures, but that didn't really tell me anything. And trying to see past the curious crowd in the delivery room hadn't told me anything either.

I loved these babies—something I don't think the doctors really understood before now. I had worked hard to get them here, and I couldn't wait to be their mother, to care for them, to feed them, to hold them.

After the aide wheeled me to Primary Children's, I was taken to the NICU floor where the girls were being cared for. We stopped at a sink so I could scrub my hands and arms. The nurse placed a mask on my face. No germs could be brought near the girls if we wanted them to survive. Then I was moved to my daughters' bedside.

They were in an open bed with a little heater hanging above them. I couldn't see them clearly. I couldn't stand for longer than a minute for fear the bleeding would start again. It was all so frustrating, but at last I got a better view of those two precious little heads and part of their body. *What is everyone talking about?* I wondered. They looked perfect and wonderful to me. They had arms and beautiful little faces. I wanted to pick them up and hold them, but there were so many tubes coming from everywhere in their body. I couldn't do anything that might put their lives in jeopardy—not now. Not ever.

No matter how much I wanted to hold them.

Instead, I touched their tiny hands and their little feet. I sat there for a few minutes, relishing the time, as I fought off the dark cloud I'd been feeling throughout the night.

"Would you like to give them a kiss?" The nurse must have read my mind.

"Yes," I'd like that," I said. "But how?"

"Let me help you," she said, offering her hand.

I stood from the wheelchair and stepped onto a stool next to the girls' encased bed. The woman helped steady me as I bent over and placed my lips against each little head for a brief moment. The wonderfulness of newborn life hit me for the first time at that moment—that perfect moment.

My babies were here; my babies were alive.

And all seemed right with the world.

CHAPTER 14

February 2002

I'd never thought when Courtney was born what a blessing it was to have your baby stay with you after the birth, not to be rushed off to the NICU. Now I knew, and I was determined I'd never take anything for granted again. Not when it came to my babies. To be able to hold them in your arms, to touch them for longer than a minute at a time, to feel their sweet breath on your cheek. All of those things are part of heaven, and as much as I was happy to have them here, I wanted even more to have them healthy.

Then the blows started to come, one right after the other, and it seemed like they might go on forever.

Kendra Deene—named after Jake's grandma, Wyllodeene Herrin—and Maliyah Mae—named after my grandma, Verna Mae—were twenty-four hours old when the doctors came to meet with us at the NICU conference room. Three doctors crowded into the room. One sat on a chair next to Jake; the other two stood leaning against the closed door.

"We've been able to examine the babies," Dr. Matlak began. He glanced at the other two doctors before he continued. "The girls are classified as Ischiopagus Type D, Omphalopagus Type B conjoined twins, meaning they are joined at the abdomen and the pelvis."

Who knows what other struggles they will face, I thought.

"The twins also share a liver, kidney, large intestine, and, of course, a single set of legs," the doctor continued. "Kendra controls one; Maliyah the other."

And the two of them controlled my heart.

"Although they seem to be healthy, their individual bodies are not complete," Dr. Matlak said. "We believe you need to sacrifice one of them, or risk the chance of losing them both."

One step at a time I reminded myself. I had thought about this before. Could I give up Maliyah for Kendra's sake? Or Kendra if it saved Maliyah's life? Jake must have thought about it, too.

"We know the odds aren't good, but we will leave the decision in the Lord's hands for right now," Jake said. "We're not going to sacrifice one for the other. We'll wait and see what He decides."

"What do we need to do to help keep them alive?" I asked.

The doctors were prepared, as though they knew we would ultimately make this decision. Dr. Matlak spoke again. "First, they will need intestinal surgery, but we must warn you, it is dangerous for premature babies. Especially your babies."

"We understand," Jake said. "How soon can you perform the operation?"

"Tomorrow," Dr. Cartwright said. "It's already on the schedule."

A warmth filled my heart. They had planned for the surgery. There must be hope the girls would again survive the night. And that was a step in the right direction.

Jake and I left the girls' hospital room, and I went back to the U of U Hospital. He went to his mom's house to get some sleep. We'd been up all night waiting to see the babies.

This was going to be a tough day for the two of us. Already I had gone through a box of tissue, crying. I was nervous and wanted to be near the babies during the surgery.

The doctors had given us the basics of what would happen. They needed to make an incision into the abdomen to create a stoma, a sort of valve using the end of the large intestine. Although the stoma might only be temporary, it was necessary if we wanted the babies to have a chance to live. The procedure took less than three hours, but to Jake and me it seemed like forever.

Once we received word the surgery was completed, I felt everything would be all right. The Lord was watching out for us, just the way I intended to watch out for the girls.

My prayers became even more fervent, if that were possible. I had always been told that it took a trial to bring people closer to the Lord, and I had discovered how true that was during the past year. Every moment we spent with Kendra and Maliyah was a blessing.

Two days later, the word from Dr. Cartwright was that only one of the girls' three kidneys was functional. *Could one of the girls have a transplant?* I began to nurture the idea and wanted to talk it over with Dr. Meyers as soon as I could.

Dr. Matlak tried to keep me informed about every change, each discovery, and all of the concerns any member of the medical team had about Kendra and Maliyah. But I wasn't prepared for the news that came when the girls were about a week old.

"Erin," one of the NICU doctors said, "I'm afraid if we don't think about separating the girls, neither one of them will ever come home from the hospital. We believe they might share a diaphragm. We can't remove the ventilator. They will have to stay in the NICU for however long . . ."

His voice had trailed off, but I knew what he meant by it—for however long they lived.

I had been released from the hospital myself and returned home. It was awkward because, although Jake was living in the basement of the house, we weren't really back together, and we didn't talk. The weeks I had spent in the hospital kept a wedge between us that seemed insurmountable. Now that I was home, Jake went right back to work, expecting me to care not only for myself, but also for Courtney, all while trying to keep abreast of what was happening with the twins. I was barely surviving emotionally, and now I had to face the decision to either separate them or watch my babies slowly die.

I picked up Courtney from my parents' house, then went home, ready to cry myself to sleep. Instead, I stayed awake all night in the master bedroom, wondering, worrying, and crying over what the doctor had told me. I wanted to talk with Jake, but I couldn't bring myself to go downstairs and let him see how upset I was. I wanted to be strong, to face everything on my own.

But I couldn't.

The next morning, I finally built up the courage to tell him what the doctor had said.

"We're not sacrificing one to save the other," Jake said.

"I know," I said, agreeing with him wholeheartedly. I loved these two little spirits, and I couldn't imagine one without the other.

Over the next two weeks, as I visited the girls each day, I learned to celebrate the tiniest of joys. Their one kidney and their bowel functioned, they took five cc's of breast milk, and they continued to live. They were on ventilators, but the gentle hum and shush sounds lulled me into a sense that everything would be okay. The doctors ran tests, too many to count. Some of them showed positive results, but others were not so good.

I settled into a routine of caring for my newborn daughters as much as I could, making sure they were clean and dry, checking for tiny bed-sores, and keeping them fed. It was satisfying to know that I was being their mom, regard-less of the circum-stances.

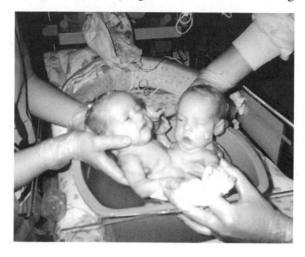

As I was nurs-ing the girls one afternoon, Dr. Mey-ers walked into the room. She sat down and began, "The girls share a single func-tioning kidney and, although one person can live with a single kidney if need be, we don't believe this is possible for two. If you decide to separate the twins . . ."

"I'll donate a kidney," I said. "I'll give them both." I would do what-ever I needed to keep these babies alive now that they had already beat-en the odds and were here.

"Your kidney will be too large for either little body," Dr. Meyers told me, "at least right now."

"Whichever girl needs it, it's hers," I assured her. "Anytime."

"The kidney is on Kendra's side, so Maliyah will likely need the transplant. It might be four or five years before she's old enough," Dr. Meyers said.

My heart sank. I tried to imagine what the girls would look like then. How big would they be? Could they survive that long?

"And no one has ever tried separating twins who depend on a single kidney," Dr. Meyers said. "Maliyah would be on dialysis until we could find a suitable donor."

How long can the single kidney support my daughters, I wondered. If it failed, could we do a transplant at this age with them anyway? What about the other organs they shared? Their liver was also a great concern because without enough bile ducts the girls would never be able to be separated. I hoped I'd be able to care for them.

After another five weeks passed in the hospital for the twins, they were finally classified as "feeders and growers," a wonderful term that meant at last they were growing and there were no major issues—well, other than the fact they were conjoined.

CHAPTER 15

April 2002

Nearly two months had passed since the twins were born. I was eager to bring them home and make them a part of the family, and at last that was going to happen. Jake and I were required to stay the night with them before the doctors and staff would release the girls to us. They called it a 'room in,' and it was our task to show them all that we had learned about caring for these very special babies.

We had full charge of the girls—feeding them, taking care of their shared body, doing everything we would need to do at home to keep them growing and making progress. This was our last chance to have nurses right there with us in case we had any new questions about the babies' care, or if there was a problem.

As far as I could see, the only problem was that there was one hospital bed, and both Jake and I would need some sleep. We knew it would be a long time before we'd again have the chance.

Kendra and Maliyah had us up most of the night. It took us two

hours to change and feed them, then we slept for an hour or so before we had to do it all again. We had to be on top of everything—know it all. Nurses and aides have so many patients to deal with, and even though these professionals can be wonderful and helpful, they can't do it all. When we got the girls home, they wouldn't be there to help us anyway.

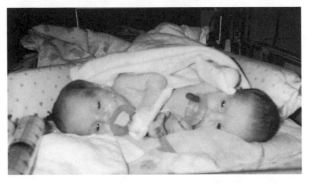

During this final night in the hospital, we had to listen, learn, ask questions and give suggestions. We learned that sometimes we needed to make a demand or two. We had that right whenever we felt we needed it.

In the morning, we felt comfortable about taking the girls home. We'd spent the last week getting everything ready. I'd not made any plans or real preparations before this past week because I'd been so uncertain that this day would ever come. What if I had prepared and they hadn't lived? It would have been too much for me to come home to a decorated, yet empty room.

We'd arranged for a crib, and my friends and I had been busy making some specially fitted clothes for the girls. We made a couple of baby blankets and got an infant carrier for the car. If the babies continued to thrive, I knew we'd need a car seat, but for now they could lay together in the carrier.

All the nurses who had cared for the twins during their time in the NICU came to say good-bye. One nurse took a photo of Jake and me

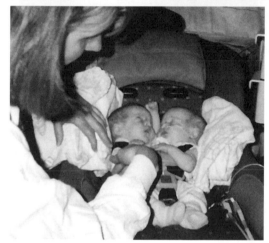

with the girls, right before we left the hospital. The girls looked so cute in their sleeper and hats. Everything matched; even the blankets. I wanted them to look as much like any other set of twins leaving the hospital as possible.

We carried them down to the car in their carrier. Jake really wanted to keep us together as a family now, and he was doing everything he could to prove it to me. We had both been living in the house for the last while, but now we'd need to be upstairs and together again so that we were both available to care for the girls throughout the night.

This next step was new for all of us—not just the girls.

CHAPTER 16

April 2002

Our house became a constant parade of friends and family who came over to help me during the day while Jake was at work. Jake's mom and sisters were wonderful, and I needed every bit of their help in just the diapering and feeding alone. They also understood that I needed some time off from the constant stress, allowing me time to meet Jake for lunch, shop, or go to church.

It was a lot of work to care for the babies and Courtney. She was only two-and-a-half and needed so many things herself. There was much to do. As parents, we had the responsibility to ensure that no one made a critical mistake—especially ourselves. We'd been there every step of the way through the pregnancy and birth, and now we'd need to train our families, even Courtney, about what to do.

But the main job would still fall on the two of us to take care of the children. There were medical supplies and equipment to arrange for and have delivered, a schedule set up for giving the girls their medications, and feeding and clothing them was more difficult than it had been with Courtney.

Grandma Patsy and her sister Marilyn invented clothes for the girls by cutting the chest out of one set and sewing the remaining pieces together into a single sleeper or outfit. Luckily, the girls were small enough at this stage we got diapers that were a size bigger than a newborn would usually need. For now the carrier we had would work in the car, but we had to find a stroller that the girls' heads would fit.

Adjusting to having these new babies was not easy for Courtney either. She became jealous of all the attention the babies were getting, and so she bit Kendra's finger. It only happened once, and she was given a time-out. Courtney had always hated time-outs. She was such a busy little girl, talkative and inquisitive, so sitting still and being quiet was enough punishment to stop the misbehavior.

She didn't really understand that there was anything different about Kendra and Maliyah. They were just her sisters, and when she wasn't feeling left out and jealous, she would sit and talk to them. Sometimes she even got to hold them, like any other big sister might do.

Unfortunately, we didn't know everything about caring for these little girls, and a week after they got home from the hospital they had to go back because they had a urinary tract infection. Antibiotics are wonderful things, and while the girls healed, I learned even more about caring for their little body.

Of course, all of the time needed to care for the twins, on top of taking care of Courtney, meant very little sleep for both Jake and me, even though there was one good result from being forced to spend all of this time working together. These little girls were bringing the two of us closer together. We discovered we were more in love than we had ever been, and a physical relationship redeveloped that would be key in saving our marriage.

But with everything, there was always the same question haunting me—would my girls ever be separated?

I'd grown tired of adults always asking me that same question, then probing further, asking what organs and body parts they shared.

The comments from the neighborhood children didn't bother me. They came running up all excited when we took our first trip to the park. They thought all twins came conjoined like Kendra and Maliyah. In their innocence about twins, they accepted the girls as being normal.

But the comments and questions from their parents and others— I couldn't stand any more. I finally got really good at answering those kind of questions: First, I would act dumb and pretend I had no idea what they meant. When they asked if the girls would be separated, I said, "I don't know. What do you think?"

For some reason, people didn't seem to understand that their prying questions were so rude that they deserved any answer I gave them. And their prying eyes and judgmental looks were no better.

But most of the time, being outside with the girls wasn't a big deal. We played in the park, and I would swing with them; however they did spend a lot of time in their stroller. Even at only eight pounds, they gave my arms and back a good workout when I tried to carry them. In the stroller, I could manage a little better, keep track of Courtney, and protect the girls from those who stared. I was never embarrassed by my girls, but I was angry at the way strangers behaved around them. I managed to block most of those people out.

Even the time the girls spent in their crib was sometimes difficult. If one of them moved an arm or leg and bumped into the other one, she was startled and occasionally got upset. If they were fussy, they didn't sleep well until we discovered a way to prop them up so they didn't roll.

Everything was exhausting, and as the girls grew, we still needed help. We couldn't do it all alone. Jake had to return to work and our extended family members had lives and obligations of their own. We wanted to do whatever we could to take care of our little family, but that left one more burden on our hearts.

Once again, I began to pray.

When Kendra and Maliyah were five-and-a-half months old, we were approached by Debbie Worthen, a local television reporter, who happened to be a cousin to Jake's brother-in-law and knew about our girls. Another set of twins—twenty-nine year-old young women—in Iran were getting ready to have separation surgery, but they died.

Debbie wanted to do a story on Utah's own twins.

When we first knew that our babies were conjoined, Jake and I discussed how much we wanted to share with anyone outside of our family. We had learned so much from the articles we had read online about other conjoined twins, but we weren't sure we wanted to bring that kind of attention to our own babies. Privacy was important, not only for the girls, but for us as a couple during what were already stressful times.

Since we didn't know if the babies would even survive, we hadn't planned for extensive media coverage. I'd been praying for some time about this very question. Would media coverage be too much of a disruption? How would it affect us as a family? Once the girls were older, would they be upset that we'd put their story on TV?

Things were going better at home, and the girls seemed to be doing fine. Debbie explained that viewers would be touched by the story, and there might be offers to help with some of our medical expenses and other needs. We hadn't worried about money, but we didn't know what the future might bring.

Jake and I talked it over and decided to let Debbie run a story, just to see where it took us. I really didn't think people would make much of it, after all, we were just a young family from Utah, and our girls happened to need separation surgery.

The next few months didn't get any easier, although the routine became familiar.

When the girls were seven months old, I wanted to play the piano for a few minutes. I had put them on the couch and tucked pillows all around them to keep them in place. My guess is they decided to work together and shove their feet against the back of the couch because the next thing I knew, they were flipped over and laying on the floor.

At first I didn't think anything was wrong, other than their being startled at the feat. But when it comes to falls, distance isn't necessarily important to produce a massive result. Maliyah cried when I picked them up. And she kept crying over the next two days whenever I touched her leg.

Two days later, I took them in to see the doctor, and we discovered that Maliyah's leg was broken. The doctor stabilized it with a splint. Kendra didn't cry because her leg was fine. Obviously, there were some places where the girls didn't share pain.

By the time winter had set in, Courtney was enrolled in dance classes and loving it. Dance gave her a chance to do something that made her feel special, and all signs of jealousy faded away. I was glad to see her so happy. The concern that I wasn't paying enough attention to her constantly nagged at me.

One afternoon, I had dropped Courtney off for dance and returned home through the slush and snow. My shoes were wet as I came into the house and walked across the tiled floor. I had decided to put the twins on the couch in the family room downstairs and had almost reached the bottom when my feet slipped out from under me.

Mother's instinct kicked in, and I managed to protect the girls from being hurt. Unfortunately, I couldn't say the same for myself. I knew I had bruised my tailbone, a fact that was proven when Jake got home from work. He gave me a friendly swat on the rear when I told him what had happened, and I started to cry. He felt bad because he hadn't realized that I really had hurt myself in such a short fall.

But when it came to the girls, if one needed to go to the hospital, they both had to go. And that's where they spent their first birthday, in the hospital, on ventilators with an upper respiratory infection.

CHAPTER 17

August 2004

The second year with the twins found Jake and me wanting to move closer to our family and the hospitals. I don't know why we hadn't thought about it before—well, actually we had thought about it, but we hadn't been able to afford the move before now.

Once we could afford it, we started looking for a lot where we could build. It took the next six months to find one in a brand new subdivision in North Salt Lake. The view was spectacular, but the best part would be the shortened commute, especially when the girls were in the hospital, a place we knew they would likely spend a great deal of time throughout their entire lives. It would take several months before the house would be done, but at least we were making progress.

During all of this time, Maliyah and Kendra's condition was not the only health issue we worried about. Jake's dad had been battling Parkinson's for over ten years, and it was moving him toward the final stages of his life. It is a horrible disease that found him losing muscular control while maintaining a clear mind.

Lamar hadn't been able to talk clearly since right before Courtney was born. It had been hard on him and hard on Jake who hadn't been able to hear words of wisdom from his dad during the times he had needed him most—finding out about Courtney, our marriage, then separation, and the birth of the twins.

As the end neared, Dad was unable to open his eyes without prying them open with his fingers. He even had difficulty swallowing. We knew his death would be a blessing, though it would be hard on everyone.

Patsy had been nearly his sole caregiver, and it was extremely difficult on her, watching her husband of forty-four years struggle for every breath. As sad as it might seem to be, his difficulties blessed us in ways we couldn't have predicted. We often wonder if maybe Grandpa chose to go to help his family, especially these two little girls.

When Grandpa Lamar left us, Patsy was prepared to help with Kendra and Maliyah. At least Patsy didn't have to be completely alone. Jake and I had sold our previous home, and it would be some time yet before the new one was ready for us to move in. So we all came to live with Grandma Patsy.

It was crazy; it was crowded; but it was nice having Jake's mom right there to help us, and she assured me that she appreciated us being so close while she dealt with her own grief.

CHAPTER 18

November 2004

With all the stress I'd been under since finding out about the girls being conjoined, my periods had been regular. Until this month when one hadn't come at all. I'd waited, thinking maybe I had miscounted the days, but when I finally broke down and bought the pregnancy test kit, the result was positive. I could hardly bear to tell Jake the news.

"You're kidding me," he said.

I shook my head. "Afraid not."

I called the obstetrician, and there was no way he was taking any chances this time. At eight weeks, I was already in for an ultrasound. The news was even more shocking.

"Looks like a set of twins," the sonogram technician said.

I know my face must have gone deathly pale. "Are they conjoined?" I wasn't sure if I wanted to hear the answer.

"No, Erin," she said. She knew me from all the times I had been in for Kendra and Maliyah, so she wasn't surprised that I would ask. "They are in different sacs, so they are fraternal."

Tears started to roll down my cheeks. How we were ever going to care for another set of twins? At only two, Maliyah and Kendra were already so much work, and Courtney was not much more than a toddler herself at four. And now we would be adding two more children?

How was I going to give Jake this news? He hadn't been able to break away from work to come to the hospital with me this time, and I knew he'd freak out when I told him about another set of twins.

I couldn't stop myself from crying. Dr. Esplin was out of town, so a different doctor was on call, a woman. The technician paged her to my room. She tried to help me calm down, understanding why I would be overwhelmed by the thought of two more babies.

"You don't have to go on with this pregnancy, you know," she said, her voice hushed and meant to be soothing.

Why would she say something like that to me? "I didn't terminate the last pregnancy, so why would I even consider ending this one?"

"I was offering you the option," she said.

I tried different ways to tell Jake about the new babies, but nothing seemed right. It didn't matter, the moment I called him I blurted the news out. "We're expecting twins."

He reacted, just like I thought he would. "Is someone trying to kill me?"

I wondered the same thing myself during the entire pregnancy. Because of the vertical C-section with the girls, my stomach muscles were not strong enough to hold the new set of babies. I had to sit down a lot, and I couldn't lift or carry any of the girls.

Other than that, everything seemed to be going well with the pregnancy. The doctors weren't worried about complications, and everyone thought I had a good chance to deliver them at thirty-six weeks. They could only hope for more time than that.

I had a tinge of concern though about my uterus. Would it hold the additional weight and keep this set of babies—I'd been able to see they were boys—safe until time to deliver?

This set of twins wasn't my only worry. Jake and I had been discussing plans for separation surgery for the girls. The doctors had wanted to see them a little stronger, a little healthier before we set a definite target date, but we felt that couldn't be too far off.

They had already accomplished things no one ever thought they would be able to. In the past few weeks, they had managed to pull themselves to a standing position, despite the way their bodies were joined. Now they could use a walker to get around some on their own. They worked together well.

The surgeons had started to talk about the separation as a possibility. There was no way I wanted to face their surgery while facing another multiple birth. Maliyah would need one of my kidneys as soon as she recovered, but I would also be in the recovery stage, and nursing.

How could any of us ever manage?

We just would, I decided. And everything would be fine.

Chapter 19

June 2005

At twenty-four weeks, I began to doubt my optimism.

The thought that I was going to die, or at least come close to dying, crossed my mind then planted itself in my brain. I couldn't shake it, so I started taking more precautions. I called a local women's group leader at my church and requested help. I needed someone else to lift the girls for me. I couldn't take the chance of rupturing anything.

I prayed the boys and I were going to make it, and that all would be well.

The afternoon of the 10th, I had an appointment for a non-stress test at the doctor's office. Since this was a high risk pregnancy, the obstetrician wanted to monitor the boys closely.

The test took around thirty minutes—a welcome break for me. I lay on the gurney, monitors strapped to my abdomen while the technician watched the twins for movement, fluid levels, and heart rate changes.

"Everything looks great," she assured me when the test was over.

I had a smile on my face as I climbed in the car. Everything was okay.

About half-way home I had a little cramp in my stomach, but I laughed it off. My pants had started to feel tight, so at a stop light I undid the tie and slipped the front down to release the pressure against my skin.

I pulled into the drive around five o'clock, just as Jake was getting home. We both went into the house. I was uncomfortable and wanted to sit down. Jake called out to his mom so that she and the kids would know we were home. I could hear them playing in the other room as I eased onto the couch recliner.

"Okay," his mom called in return. "See you at the birthday party in a little while." I heard the door close behind her as she left for her own house.

That's when the intense pains started. I wrapped my arm under my belly, thinking that if I held the babies in place the pain would go away.

"Jake, I think something is wrong," I said. I gritted my teeth and tears came to my eyes. "I hurt really bad."

"Go lie down," Jake said. "I'll bring you some pain pills."

"Bring more than two," I said.

But I couldn't walk, the pains were so strong, and Jake ended up having to help me into the bedroom. I was crying, but I took the pills, hoping they would work fast. I lay down, trying to give the medicine a chance. Jake stayed with me, and I guess the kids sensed I didn't feel well because they stayed quiet in the other room.

Suddenly, I knew this was more serious than a severe cramp. "Jake," I said. "We need to go to the hospital now!"

He gave me a look that seemed to say, "Are you sure?"

I was sure. The pain suddenly reached about a twenty on a scale of ten. I think Jake could read the panic cross my face because he immediately started moving toward getting me out of the house and into the car. We would have to take the kids to Patsy's house before we could go to the hospital. It was a blessing she only lived five minutes away. Since she was hosting a party for Jake's nephew, we knew there would be plenty of people there, ready to help take care of our kids, too.

"I don't want to die," I said as I got into the car.

"You won't," Jake said.

"I love you," I said. "And I love all the kids." I was in such pain I could hardly stand it, but I felt I needed to tell him over and over again how I felt, as though this were my last goodbye. "I want you to do everything you can to save the boys."

I needed something to take my mind off the pain's intensity, so I started singing *I Am a Child of God* to myself. The song was one I sang often to the twins, and it was among Courtney's favorites.

I could feel myself slipping into shock as the intensity of the pain increased. Parts of my body felt numb, but my abdomen felt like it was being ripped from me. Breathing became a chore, and everything seemed out of focus. Sweat was pouring off me by the time we reached the hospital.

Jake pulled the car up to the entrance of LDS Hospital, threw it into park, turned off the ignition and ran inside to get a wheelchair. I couldn't get out of the car, I hurt so bad, Jake had to pick me up and put me in the chair. Since he knew what floor Labor and Delivery were on, he rushed my wheelchair toward the elevators and took me directly there.

"He stopped at the desk at the front of the floor. "My wife's in terrible pain."

"You'll need to fill out this paperwork," the nurse said.

I grabbed the papers and threw them back at her. "You've got to take me now," I demanded. I knew I couldn't wait to be taken into the delivery room. "My uterus is ripping! I need a doctor, immediately!"

One of the older nurses could tell I meant business. She jumped up, taking charge. Both the babies and I were in trouble, and she knew it.

"Follow me," she said to Jake, as she grabbed the handles on my wheelchair and headed toward an examination room. Immediately I was surrounded by nurses, pulling at my clothes to get me undressed and into a hospital gown.

Jake stood there, not sure what he was supposed to do. I was moved to an examination table, an ultrasound machine seemed to appear out of nowhere, and the technician squirted the gel onto my belly. Even that caused pain.

After a few minutes, which the pain made feel like hours, the tech said, "I don't see a tear, and we've got both babies' heartbeats. I think everything is okay."

"Well, I don't think so," I shouted. I could feel my stomach catch as another intense shot of pain passed through it.

"Let's try a different kind of monitor," she said.

Once it was hooked up, one baby's heart rate dropped to the sixties. The nurse double-checked it against the ultrasound and said, "We need to get her into delivery, immediately!"

I heard her mention a C-section, but I didn't care about anything. I knew I was dying.

They moved me to a bed, poked an IV into my arm and wheeled me into surgery, leaving Jake behind. Once in the delivery room, they washed my belly off with soap, and I screamed because the pain was so severe.

"Please, please help me," I begged.

"That's what we're doing, Erin," the anesthesiologist said as he slipped the mask over my nose.

At 6:15 p.m., I delivered two little boys—one weighing only three pounds eight ounces and the other four pounds two ounces—but the next thing I remember was waking up with Jake, his mom, and my sister, Heidi, standing by me. I saw the transfusion bag hanging next to the IV drip, and both of them had tubes leading into me.

The intense pain had been the rupture of my uterus, and the pain wasn't completely over. When the nurse came to check on me, she touched my abdomen and it hurt so bad tears came streaming down my face. I don't think she had any idea of how much I hurt.

"The boys are fine," Jake told me.

I took a breath and thanked my Father in Heaven.

We named our sons Justin Erron Jeffrey, a combination of my dad's and my name, and Austin Jacob Lamar after Jake and his dad.

"I feel bad I didn't carry them full term," I said. "Are the doctors sure the twins will be okay?"

"Yes, it was you we were worried about," Dr. Esplin said as he entered the room. He had come to check on me. His face was somber, so I knew he was serious. "A fifteen minute delay anywhere and you could have died from the loss of blood. Your uterus was split all the way open and amniotic fluid was everywhere in the abdomen. You were lucky you made it to the hospital."

The Lord was with me. And He was with the boys.

A couple of days after they were born, the nurse came to see me. She was young and didn't know anything about me. "You'll need to pump sixty ounces of milk each day."

She was so matter of fact about it, but I doubted she'd ever had a baby. I'd never had trouble with the pump for Kendra and Maliyah, and they were more stressful than having these boys. I was able to pump eighty-plus ounces a day for them. The freezer had been overflowing then, and I didn't think it would be difficult with these two.

I spent a week in the hospital with Justin and Austin. Once again, it was hard not to take my children home from the hospital with me. I had expected this with Kendra and Maliyah, but not this time around.

I was sick in bed for eight days after I got home. I don't know what bug I had picked up. Maybe it was nerves about the next stage of our lives.

Because they were premature, the babies spent the first three weeks in the NICU where we began to notice how much each of them looked like their grandfather namesake. We had chosen correctly and couldn't be more proud of our brand new boys.

Our house was already crazy, but now it would become insane. Jake and I had five children, all under the age of five.

And two of them needed separation surgery.

CHAPTER 20

January 2006

Jake and I had started discussing the possibilities of separating Kendra and Maliyah with the doctors right after the girls were born, but the surgeons had concerns about the effectiveness of the girls' organs. Could they survive alone?

Once a year the girls had a CT scan. We met with the surgeon and discussed the possibility of separation. Dr. Sherbotie was concerned that the girls might hit a growth spurt which could be too much for their single kidney, yet he understood the problems that would come before Maliyah could receive one.

Finally, we were greeted with good news.

"The new CT scan proves that their liver is divided. We can see it clearly," Dr. Meyers told us when the girls turned four. "It will be safe to separate them. We can get started with the preliminaries this week."

This week? I couldn't believe it. Neither Jake nor I said anything, despite the fact the doctor kept looking back and forth between the two of us. I know she expected a decision. Did we still want to separate them? Of course we did, but even with all the time we'd had to think about it, it suddenly seemed too quick.

"I think we need to go home and think things through," Jake said. "We have to make sure this is the right choice for the girls."

I knew that was Jake's cue that we needed to pray about it one more time. I felt the same way, and I knew the sense of shock I felt right now wasn't letting me think clearly.

"Kendra has her Make-a-Wish trip to Florida this week," I said.

"Then let's talk again about it when you return," the doctor said. "Give my office a call, and we'll set up an appointment right away."

We left the office, agreeing that was what we would do.

I knew that separation was the right thing. Kendra and Maliyah were two very distinct and individual personalities. We wanted the girls to be able to live the most normal lives possible, to make their own choices and be able to live them through. We wanted to give them the chance to live and grow as individuals.

But we also never wanted them to forget about the time they were conjoined.

In the end, it was Maliyah and Kendra who helped us finalize our decision. Of course, we would never let them make the decision, because if something went wrong with either of them, they would feel responsible. That burden needed to fall on me and Jake alone. We discussed the surgery with the two of them, and what kinds of changes it would mean in their lives. We wanted to know what they wanted and how they saw themselves.

"You mean, I can be playing on the computer while Maliyah plays with Barbies in the other room?" Kendra asked one day.

"Can we sleep in our own beds?" Maliyah wanted to know..

When I told them yes, they said they were ready. Of course they loved being together, but this idea of being two girls gave them so many more possibilities of things they could do.

And they wanted those opportunities, although they did wonder about the pain it might bring.

I worried about that too. And I knew it might be more than just physical.

The final question would be, *was I ready?*

CHAPTER 21

❧❧

January 2006

When the girls had turned three, we heard about the Make-a-Wish Foundation and decided to apply for a wish for each of them before they underwent separation surgery. We didn't know if their wishes would be granted, but I filled out the referral forms and sent them in. We thought their chances seemed pretty good when the foundation contacted the girls' doctor to get their medical background and to discuss their future.

We were so relieved when the foundation contacted us at last about sending out their representative to discuss possible wishes for the girls.

Maliyah is very shy, so I knew something at home would be the best thing for her. I had gone to a recent Parade of Homes and saw a castle in one of the little girl's room that I knew Maliyah would love. That would be her wish.

Kendra is a lot more outgoing, so I knew she would love to take her sister to Disney World. The Make-A-Wish rep filled out the paperwork, and again we waited, but not for long. A few weeks later, we had our answer. Yes.

But that didn't mean the wish was ready to be granted. Maliyah's castle would be the first wish granted, but this organization wanted it to be a day to remember. We had some remodeling to do, and the girls couldn't know anything about what was going on in our basement.

Over the next few months, Jake worked hard at getting the playroom done so the Make-a-Wish foundation could send over an artist to do something special. Dave, the artist they sent, had a son who suffered from a brain tumor. He had been the recipient of a wish, and his dad wanted to give back to another family. Dave spent nearly forty hours painting a mural on our wall, setting the perfect scene to accompany the castle.

The day of the unveiling party, we had thirty or forty guests come to the house, including people from the foundation. I had dressed the girls in princess outfits, although they didn't know why at first.

Until we took them into the new room in the basement.

"Mommy, a castle!" Maliyah said. I could tell both girls were excited.

"Yes, sweetheart," I said. "Your castle." I wiped back the tears from my eyes.

"Your majesties," one of the Make-a-Wish people said as she placed a crown on their heads. The girls loved princesses, and now they both had their chance to be one.

Of course, the highlight of the day was when the girls had Courtney kiss a frog. Yucky! But everyone laughed.

A few days later, we were on our way to the Disney Resorts for Kendra's wish. It was the girls' first time to fly, and they both cried. I know the change in air pressure had to hurt their little ears more than it did mine.

When we got to Orlando, we were met by hosts arranged by Make-a-Wish to make our trip easier. They held a huge Give Kids the World poster so we would know who they were, and they gave the kids each some candy to suck on while we went to ground transportation where our luggage was. We were not the only family here for a special wish, and this group certainly knew how to take care of us all.

We were taken to a cottage sponsored by the Florida organization, and the girls immediately dubbed the place our "pretend home." Every day we were taken to a different one of the resort parks, then at night the group held a special party where they brought in favorite characters to entertain all the children who were there. The twins had asked if Dora the Explorer could come to their party. Even though she isn't a Disney character, the group made sure she was there.

Another highlight of the trip was the day we went to Disney World itself. Maliyah was enthralled by the castle and everyone enjoyed the show where they crowned Cinderella. After the show, I went over to one of the workers and asked if we could meet the princess. She told us no, but seconds later I was approached by one of the managers.

"My girls would like to meet Cinderella," I said, pointing at the stroller where Kendra and Maliyah sat.

"Meet me behind the castle, and I'll bring her to you," he promised.

We went where he had instructed, and he met us there. "Come on in," he said as he held open a door. We entered a large room that had been painted like the inside of a castle.

Then he did something more than introduce us to Cinderella. Snow White and her Prince, Jasmine and Aladdin, Belle and the Beast, Sleeping Beauty, the King, a Fairy Godmother, and Prince Phillip all came into the room to meet Kendra and Maliyah. It was so beautiful and touching that both Jake and I cried, overcome with emotion.

After we had met everyone, they had us return to the front of the castle and take seats to watch the show again. This time when the characters started singing and dancing, they blew kisses and waved at the girls who absolutely loved it.

The wish had definitely been one to remember.

The Herrins with all the Disney Princes and Princesses
at Disney World, Florida

CHAPTER 22

June 2006

Kendra and Maliyah were admitted to the hospital at the end of June, about six weeks before the scheduled separation surgery. The doctors had explained it would be necessary to insert a series of tissue expanders. This involved implanting seventeen inflatable balloons under the girls' skin where the doctors would need excess tissue to close the wound after the separation. It would take several weeks of saline injections and increasing the balloons' inflation to slowly stretch their skin. The tension causes new cells to form, making the skin grow.

Once the expanders were in place, the girls could not leave the hospital. They had to spend most of their time in a special bed and mattress filled with soft sand meant to keep them from damaging their new skin. Even with this extra precaution, there were still problems and the surgery had to be postponed a week because the skin over one expander was slow to heal.

But the time at the hospital also had its special memories.

Once I was visiting with someone in the girls' room and talking about Jake's grandma Wyllodeene. She had died in March of 2002 while the girls were in the NICU, so the girls had never known her.

Suddenly, Kendra piped up, "I know Grandma Wyllodeene."

"No, sweetie," I assured her. She knew that Kendra was named after this grandma, but there was no way she knew her. "She's been gone a long time."

"She was here yesterday," Kendra insisted. "She comes at night and kneels by our bed to pray."

I didn't know what to say. Surely the veil between life and death was thin for my precious children. Who could guess what they might actually see that I might never see?

Grandma Wyllodeene wasn't the only special visitor the girls had, although the others were definitely in this realm and not from the great beyond. Classmates from school and church, along with friends and family—even members of the hospital staff— stopped in to see the twins and to let us know they were praying for them as well.

Grandma Patsy watched Courtney and the boys most of the days while I spent time with the girls at the hospital. Grandma Patsy loved helping with them all and found it easier and more relaxing than caring for Grandpa Lamar before he died.

Of course there were other people helping as well, and the children's lives went on as though everything were normal. Courtney had her dance lessons, and the boys were growing like crazy as they moved from infant to toddler.

Someone from the Disney organization knew about the upcoming surgery from a television news report, and they had all the characters we had met that special morning at Disney World autograph a poster which they sent to the hospital. It now hung on the wall so the girls could look at it and remember their special day.

The psychologist tried to prepare the girls mentally while Dr.

Meyers and her team monitored their progress physically. The child-life specialist had made a set of dolls that were conjoined, one for each girl. The doll could be separated into two when the girls were ready. Kendra cut hers apart on July 20th. Maliyah waited until right before the actual surgery in August. I had made a paper chain to help them count down the days until their own separation.

Jake and I continued to have meetings with all the doctors who would be working with the girls. We discussed the outline of procedures they would need to do and about how long they expected each to take. I felt like I was going to medical school non-stop, but I wanted to know everything. I'd never anticipated my high school goal to pursue medicine as coming true like this.

The media didn't give us any kind of relief either. They tried everything short of breaking down doors to get to us or other members of our family for an interview, a sound bite, any little inkling of information about the girls and their upcoming surgery.

As anyone who has ever been in the news might know, one story is never enough to satisfy the public. The only thing I wanted from all the attention was for someone who read about us to investigate our Church, so we told people it was our LDS faith that helped us remain so strong. It was true. All those days I had spent doing sessions in the temple before the twins were born had solidified the way I felt about the Church and the Lord.

Everyone wanted permission to cover the story. But I was scared. What if something happened to the girls? I didn't want everyone to see how much pain we were in. I wanted my privacy—not a show for the world.

CHAPTER 23

August 2006

On the day before the surgery—a Sunday—Jake and I arrived at the hospital very early with Courtney so all three girls could spend the day together. We wanted it to be a special day for everyone, but it was very emotional for Jake and me. We both cried most of the day.

In the evening, family members came to the hospital to see the girls. Jake asked all the worthy priesthood holders who were there to assist him in giving the twins a blessing. My brother-in-law, Big Jorge, and my dad anointed their heads with special consecrated oil, then Jake gave the actual blessing. The words he spoke are too precious to share, but before he was through, tears were streaming down his face.

"That was the most powerful feeling I've ever had while giving a blessing," he said.

Everyone in the room could feel it, too.

After the blessing, Patsy took Courtney, Justin, and Austin home with her. Jake and I knew we were going to spend the night with the twins, so we had brought air mattresses which we set up next to their bed. Neither one of us slept very well, but the girls did.

⌒⌒

At 5:45 a.m. we were up and started getting ready for the big day. We awoke Kendra and Maliyah, wanting to hold them for the last time as conjoined twins.

"Is it Cut-Apart Day?" Kendra asked almost immediately.

"Today is the day," I said, hoping she wasn't worried, like I was.

I'm not sure worried is a strong enough word to describe how I felt. Terrified might be better. My nerves were raw, my emotions ready to erupt every second. I tried to stay positive so the girls wouldn't see how upset I was and become frightened themselves. If anything went wrong today—if I lost one or both of my precious daughters—I'd never be able to live with myself.

We had asked to be alone with the girls as long as possible. The past few days had been hard on them. They had been so scared when Dr. Rockwell and Dr. Siddiqi, the plastic surgeons, came in to mark the spots for surgery that they cried and cried. This morning, I wanted the girls to remain calm and my own heart to be at ease.

After a little while, I took them to the window and let them look outside. The area was surrounded by camera trucks and news people stood on the lawn, talking into microphones about the surgery that was to take place soon—*my children's surgery*. We'd asked so many times how they felt about being on television and becoming famous.

"Will we be like Dora the Explorer?" Kendra had asked.

"Just as famous," I told her.

The two of them had looked at each other and nodded. They thought that would be okay.

But this morning, the girls didn't care about all the media attention. I wanted nothing more than to ignore it myself, so I moved away from the window.

For years, ever since they could understand, we'd been preparing the girls for this day. I was afraid to let them go, uncertain what would come from this surgery. The separation would be the scariest thing I had ever done. None of the surgeries they'd undergone to correct problems since they were born even came close.

I suppose some would find it odd, but I was sad that I would never see the girls conjoined again. I'd grown so used to holding them both together that I couldn't imagine how I would feel afterward. Of course, I knew what it was like to hold twins, one on each arm instead of together. I had Justin and Austin, after all.

"Who do you want to see first when you wake up from the surgery?" I asked them, fighting hard to keep a light tone in my voice.

"Dad," Kendra said.

"Mom," Maliyah added.

"Okay," I said. I hadn't been surprised by their choices. It was the way it had always been.

When it was time, Jake and I walked toward the operating room with the girls. We both told them how much we loved them and how we wanted the very best for them, assuring them that the Lord and His angels would watch over them.

"We aren't doing this because there is something wrong with you," I said, hoping to assure them. "We love you and know how much you will want this once you are older. We want you to be safe." I started to cry, but I had more that I wanted to tell them. "Don't you worry about anything because Mom will worry about everything."

I must say it was not easy taking my little girls into surgery like this. There were so many variables—so much that could go wrong—so many risks. My commitment didn't waver because I knew it was for their good, but knowing that didn't make it any easier. I was having trouble seeing, the tears fell so hard.

The trip down the hall toward surgery took several minutes because the staff had decorated the corridor with little flip-posters to celebrate the girls' differences. Anything that made Kendra and Maliyah each feel unique was part of the display, and the gurney stopped at every poster so the girls could look at each one: caterpillars, butterflies, all their favorite things.

Everything was going smoothly, despite my sobbing. The girls were in good spirits. Then we reached the door where they would go on and Jake and I would be left behind.

"I don't want to go! Let us stay with you!" The girls had suddenly changed their minds, and the uncertainty of the moment came crashing through the smiles they had worn only minutes earlier.

"Oh, Jake," I said, turning to my husband. "This is the hardest thing I've ever done."

"I know," he said. "But it's the best thing for them."

I tried to reassure them that everything was going to be all right and after nearly twenty minutes they calmed down. I held each little face in my hands for a minute, rubbing my nose against theirs in an Eskimo kiss. Jake did the same. Then I kissed each girl on the forehead and whispered, "Goodbye."

"This is not goodbye." Dr. Meyers had come from the operating room to comfort us. "This is just 'see you later.'"

At 7:00 a.m., Jake and I stood together, my arms around him, both of us crying as we watched the cart take our conjoined twins away from us for the very last time. The thought came to me so strongly: *Why am I crying? I know the outcome.* I knew what was going to happen because they were given a blessing that said their surgery would be successful, and they would bless many people's lives around them. But I couldn't help but wonder a tiny bit if they would be alive to do that.

I had to have faith that the next time we saw them, they would have two separate bodies, and Kendra and Maliyah would be smiling.

CHAPTER 24

August 2006

The hours seemed like days as the surgery moved forward. Every step of the separation had been taken exactly as the doctors had outlined. Miraculously, the surprise of the pericardial sac had not added a set-back to the time schedule.

Once again, I was so grateful it was only the sac. If the girls had been joined in the heart muscle itself, it would have been all over. There would have been no way they could live, together or apart, not that far into the surgery. We would have never had them with us again.

"The surgery is going well," Dr. Matlak assured us the last time he had come out. "Everything is going to be okay. We just dodged the bullet, so to speak. Nothing to be overly concerned about now."

Right. Mothers worry about everything. What would they look like now that they were no longer conjoined? What kinds of problems might they have immediately? What might they face in the future? I could only hope—and pray.

The entire ordeal was emotionally taxing. I couldn't imagine how hard it had to be on the girls. They had the doctors—and I couldn't forget the angels—to watch after their needs. I had Jake and our extended family but that didn't prevent me from the constant ups and downs of the emotional roller coaster ride I was on.

However it did bring Jake and me even closer together.

Would the separation change the closeness Kendra and Maliyah felt for each other? I was amazed at how much they had learned to do together. They could scoot around, roll over, pull themselves up to stand, and even do a somersault. They learned something new every day, proving to us all how smart they were.

And they were best friends with such a close bond. I hoped nothing would ever come between them. I wanted them to remember being conjoined, and how special they were because they came into this world born in a perpetual hug.

At one point, when Dr. Meyers came to update us, I asked her, "What does Maliyah look like?" They had explained to us that Kendra had the best chance of retaining the lower portions of their body.

The doctor looked at me with no emotion showing on her face or in her voice when she said, "I can't see Maliyah. I see her liver, her bowel and organs, but I can't see Maliyah. I can't do surgery on Maliyah because that would be too much. I can't think about her right now." Then she walked out of the room.

My heart was crushed, but I understood what she meant. She had to distance herself, not see Maliyah as a sweet little girl if she wanted to make it through the surgery. I knew Dr. Meyers loved my daughter and was doing everything in her power to save Maliyah so I could raise her and watch her grow into a beautiful, independent woman.

Dr. Meyers understood how much we relied on her for Maliyah's safety. The separation was what was best for our precious daughter. We trusted all of the medical staff with the girls' lives, and they felt that.

They knew how much we loved them and how hard this decision was for us to make. This wasn't going to be easy, but we all could get through it—the doctors, Jake, and me.

After eighteen hours, at 11:00 p.m., the word finally came—the girls were separated. Their torso, liver, and intestines were divided; their circulatory systems rerouted. No longer did our daughters hold each other in a constant hug.

"I moved Kendra from her sister's side and took her into her own operating room." Dr. Matlak told us the news with tears in his eyes. Then he was gone, back to his duties in the next round of surgery. (Later he told us that when he had lain Kendra down on the operating table, he looked at the gaping hole in her and wondered at what he had done. How was he going to fix this? The girls were counting on him. We were counting on him. And the world was watching. It was a daunting task. He spoke of shutting his eyes and saying a prayer. Thoughts came to him as he went to work to close the wound. When he didn't know what to do next, he would pray again and the inspiration would come to him. For the next ten hours this was what he did repeatedly.)

Jake and I fell into a hug of our own. Tears poured from my eyes, and Jake cried as well. The biggest step was over. Today, at this moment, we celebrated each stage of the marathon surgery. For the first time, Kendra and Maliyah were in two rooms, and new operations were underway. The celebration was part of learning to pace ourselves. With the doctor's skill and the Lord's blessing, we would get through this. Kendra and Maliyah would survive.

In addition to being a victory for our family, the surgery was a milestone for the medical community as well. It was the first time conjoined twins sharing a single kidney were separated successfully. Kendra had retained the kidney, and Maliyah would be on dialysis until she could have a transplant. But the surgery had been done and, at this point, was a success.

Although we felt so much relief, we knew it wasn't over yet. We'd been at this since 7:00 a.m. and it was now after midnight, but the doctors had much work to do so that each girl could survive alone.

The next time Dr. Matlak came to talk with us, he said, "I'm worried there isn't enough skin to close Kendra's belly. I've performed separations before, but I've never seen an opening as massive as this." He rubbed his hands across his now-bristled face, his morning shave coming due. His eyes were red-rimmed, proving he must be tired. It had been a long day, and it was far from over.

I wondered if he was as scared as I was, but I walked into the other room to tell the rest of the family. "We need to pray," I said after explaining the doctor's concerns. "We need to pray for Kendra and for Dr. Matlak."

I had complete faith in him and his ability as a doctor. There wasn't one moment I thought he wouldn't save my little girl. I felt he was chosen to be with Kendra for a reason. He was a spiritual man, and we had constantly prayed that he was doing what was right for our beloved daughter.

But an extra prayer couldn't hurt.

We rejoined the doctor and offered the prayer together, then Dr. Matlak went back into surgery.

The girls spent another ten hours in the operating room, where the surgeons rebuilt the girls' pelvises and abdominal walls. At 5:10 a.m. the urologist, Dr. Catherine deVries, told us, "We're in the home stretch, but it will be a long one."

Finally, on the morning of August 8th, at 8:20 a.m., we received wonderful news—Maliyah was out of surgery. At 9:30 a.m., Kendra's surgery was finished as well. There had been enough skin to cover their incisions, although Kendra's was close.

They were listed in critical condition, but we would be able to see them soon.

They had come through the separation surgery, but Jake and I were concerned about what to expect when we entered their room. Was it going to be more than we could stand? The entire set of doctors came out one at a time to tell us what to prepare for. Whatever we saw, I prayed I'd be able to handle it.

Finally Dr. Meyers and Dr. Matlak came.

"When I didn't know what to do, I prayed," Dr. Matlak said. "And I felt like my movements were being guided through the surgery. We were able to use their organs to sustain life in both girls." He started crying as he was overcome by the gravity of all that had happened.

Then all the emotions Dr. Meyers had held in for those twenty-six hours came out. She cried and I cried and we hugged.

"Both girls look so good. Of course, they will have healing to do, but they are two beautiful little girls now," Dr. Meyers said through her tears. "We were able to close the wounds with new skin. The sutures will heal. I didn't expect them to look so good right after the surgery. I'm surprised and happy."

Our doctors had done it. They were the angels in the operating room who had done their very best to make our girls whole—the way the girls would see themselves when they got older. The doctors gave them a gift that we, as their parents, could never do. It was the gift of separate lives.

"There were several times we wanted to change the original plan, complete a procedure in a different order," Dr. Matlak said, "but we couldn't without causing potential complications. As it turns out, the original plan must have been inspired. If we had made any of the changes, we probably wouldn't have been able to save both girls."

Once again we knew how the Lord had touched our lives and the lives of our daughters by guiding the hands and minds of those doctors, and we couldn't be more grateful.

Tired, my concerns somewhat reassured, but still curious, I thought I was ready to enter the NICU recovery room to see my girls. The doctors tried to explain to Jake and me how the single body had been made into two, but I couldn't picture it well enough to understand exactly.

"Let's just go in," I said. "I can't wait any longer."

It was about 11:00 a.m. when I entered the recovery room. The first thing that hit me was the beds—two of them. They were on two different sides of the room. And each had an occupant.

This was a startling first for me to see my sweet little four-year-old girls, lying flat on their backs in separate beds. Because of the way they had been conjoined, Kendra and Maliyah had always been turned a little toward each other so that neither one of them had ever truly been flat against the mattress before, without her sister on top of her.

I couldn't move closer because I was sobbing so hard from the shock. In all honestly, I could barely stand, I was so overcome with emotion. This moment was bittersweet; all the years of wondering if we were ever going to see the girls separate had come to a resolution.

What I had come to know, understand, and love about our girls had changed. For one thing, Maliyah was on the left. When they were conjoined, it was Kendra on the left. It was a shock to me. When Jake took my hand and gave it a squeeze, I knew he felt the same way.

We had experienced a miracle.

"Normal little girls," Jake said, "just with one leg."

Someone had done the girls' hair into French braids, and they each now wore a bow. Maliyah's was yellow and Kendra's purple. Their favorite colors.

The doctors had made everything seem so much worse than what it really was, preparing us for the moment of seeing the girls' raw skin, new and easily damaged. Even as I took in what the girls looked like, I was thinking of how much pain they were going to be in when they awoke. I wondered where we would go from here and what my daughters' recovery would be like.

But for this very moment I was going to take in the miracle of this day. The angels had been with us from both sides of the veil, and I had never felt the spirit of the Lord as strongly as I did at that moment.

And everything was good.

CHAPTER 25

August 2006

We had promised the girls that Kendra would see Jake first, and that I'd be there for Maliyah, so we each waited at the correct bedside. A promise was a promise.

At last, they awoke enough to recognize we were there. I was relieved to see my little girls alive. They were heavily sedated and on ventilators because their bellies were tight from their organs swelling.

The concern that we had for them couldn't go away. So many things could still go wrong, and once they were no longer sedated, we didn't know how they would react to the medications. A week and a half later, we found out.

Maliyah had hallucinations. At first I thought she was joking, but as time went on they got more intense. She thought she saw masked men and ants and spiders.

The anesthesiologist had told NICU not to give Maliyah any morphine, but they had. Without a kidney, her tissue kept absorbing the meds, and it became toxic in her blood because the dialysis wasn't great at clearing the meds either. That caused the hallucinations.

The doctors assured us once the meds wore off, the frightening images would go away, but that would be a slow process because she didn't have a kidney—nothing to clear out the morphine that was making her see things. The doctors tried different combinations to control the problem, but every combination made it worse.

Maliyah needed to be back on the ventilator, but she couldn't. The doctors were afraid the pain killers would repress her breathing so much it might kill her. A nurse sat by her bed all night and helped keep her airway open so she could breathe.

During one episode, she flailed her body, tearing open a place on her back—creating another wound that would need to heal. She wasn't making as much progress as any of us would like to see, and I hadn't received suggestions yet from the plastic surgeon. My niece was a nurse, so I asked her what she thought we should do to speed up the healing process. She told me about Wound VAC, a way to close the tissue with a foam dressing until the tissue could heal. Because it was a specialized piece of equipment, it was very expensive, but I wanted the very best for my daughter. I'd worry about fighting the insurance company later.

The very next day when I went into the NICU, the surgeon was with the girls.

"What do you think of getting a Wound VAC?" I asked.

"That might be a good idea," he said. "Let's give it a try."

That afternoon the specialist from the company's distributor was there to set up the machine and put a new kind of dressing on Maliyah. We hoped to solve this problem so her body could cope with the repercussions of dialysis without the added stress of healing her wounds. The dialysis alone was much worse than what we anticipated, and the hours she spent on the machine seemed endless. It was a miracle that she lived the three days after the separation without dialysis.

The next few days as she stayed in ICU weren't much better, and the next week, the incisions along her torso ever so slowly opened up.

What kind of hell have I put these children through? I wondered.

Maliyah became despondent, refusing to look at me. No matter what I tried, she pulled her eyes away the second she sensed I was looking at her.

"Why do you think she is doing that?" I asked Jake, almost whining. "I'm her mother. Why won't she look at me?"

"I don't know," he said. "She won't look at me either."

"Do you think she might be depressed?" I worried that her health and the separation might be too hard for her to handle.

"Maybe it's the pain medications," Jake said, trying to assure me.

I sobbed all the way home, wondering what I could possibly do to help her. I needed direction from the Lord, because the only thing I knew was to keep her on the machine as long as it was necessary. The words of prayer came into my heart, but I didn't feel their immediate comfort like so many times before. I felt like I was in mourning over the girls no longer being conjoined.

Courtney must have had some of the same feelings. She had come to see them that day and everything went really well, until we got home.

"Mommy and Daddy," she said. "Why did you take them apart? I liked them how they were." She started to cry.

A few days earlier Jake whispered to Kendra "Do you know what happened to you?" Kendra responded "Yes, I'm cut apart."

"Are you okay?" Jake asked. Kendra nodded with a smile.

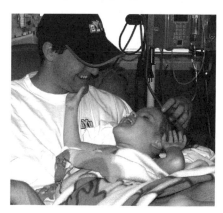

Jake and I reminded her about what we talked about before the surgery. She was thoughtful for a minute, then said she missed her sister.

"Once you're all better, you two can get in the same bed and pretend you're still stuck together." Her huge grin told me she would be okay.

It seemed Courtney needed the same kind of reassurance. She crawled into bed with Jake and me around 7:00 p.m. We all missed Maliyah and Kendra. I felt as though we had lost something so special, and we needed each other to feel whole again. Lonely for her sisters, Courtney fell asleep in our bed, and I soon followed her lead. My mind and body were both exhausted.

I guess Jake must have slept as well until around midnight, when I woke up screaming at him, "Something is wrong with the girls!" I don't know if was a mother's paranoia, or if I was too tired to make sense of anything, but I was in a panic. My heart raced and my entire body felt cold and clammy.

Jake was half asleep but still grabbed the phone and dialed the NICU. The nurse in the girls' room answered, and Jake asked, "Is everything okay?"

I could tell by the way he nodded that everything was fine, but he hung up the phone and said, "They're doing well. Everything is fine." Then he went right back to sleep.

It took me a few minutes longer, but I slept the rest of the night, waking the next morning when Courtney said, "I want them home, and I want them back together. I am going to miss playing with them conjoined."

"We feel the same way," I told her, and we cried together. It seemed to help her feel better.

The next day, I was sitting between the two beds, playing with Kendra when Maliyah's dialysis machine suddenly shut down. I glanced toward it, as though expecting to hear the rhythmic whooshing sound start up again. Her treatment was constant, and I had gotten used to the noise. The silence was deafening.

"Did something happen to the power?" I asked the nurses who were always on duty. I followed the cord with my eyes from the machine to the wall then reached over to make sure it was firmly plugged in. The machine's lights were on, but the machine itself stood silent.

Before I could ask the nurse for her opinion, an alarm went off and she moved toward it. "Looks like a blood clot caught in the filter," she said. She hit the silence button. "Let's get someone up here to check it. We'll get this sorted out. Not to worry."

Those words again. Of course I worried. Maliyah had a friend who died because they were unable to rethread her dialysis catheter. The child had only been five years old. Our family was going to do Sub-for-Santa for her, but she died.

I realized at that moment how important the dialysis machine was, yet how sick it could make someone. Once the tubing was clamped and the water forced her blood back through the dialysis catheter, Maliyah perked right up again. But another problem with the machine could suck the life right out of her if it wasn't monitored properly.

During the time the machine was turned off, Maliyah was like her old self. For the next two hours, I was able to talk and interact with her, and just be with her again while someone cleared the tubing and filters of the machine.

The tech worked on the machine for two hours, but during that time I was so grateful that it was the machine and not something I had done that caused her discomfort.

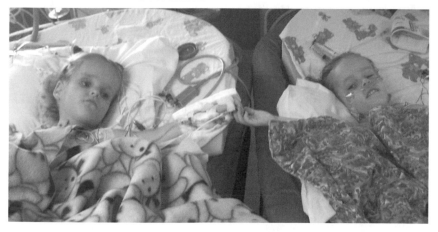

Once they were done, I begged the doctors not to put her back on dialysis for a while longer, but that wasn't possible. And my Maliyah went away—she was right back to looking at the ceiling with the blank stare that I hated so much. I knew that very moment she needed a kidney, and fast. This was no life for my baby.

I would have been happier if nothing had gone wrong, but at least now I knew something to watch out for.

And there was plenty to watch for with both of the twins. Kendra had a bowel blockage caused by scared tissue from the separation surgery, but two weeks after this surgery, she was bouncing on her bed and playing with toys. She needed very little pain medication.

Maliyah was not doing nearly as well, and two weeks after her sister, Maliyah also had a bowel obstruction that required surgery. Of course, we also worried for both girls because their fragile skin that bound the incisions began to retract more and more each day. What if the sutures pull completely apart? The skin around them was dying.

We knew Maliyah faced at least one more major surgery—a kidney transplant. Her kidney was one of the reasons why we couldn't do the separation when the girls were younger. Only a few successful kidney transplants had ever been performed on a child younger than the age of four—the ages our girls were now—and never one from conjoined twins. We had wanted to give Maliyah her best chance, and this was it. Now she just had to heal, while we seriously began the search for a donor.

We arranged for Home Health Care assistance again and prepared an upstairs bedroom. This time we would need two oxygen compressors, one for Kendra and one for Maliyah. We wanted to be ready when the doctors said we could bring them home, and we wanted to take both girls there at the same time.

At last, the blood work showed both of their conditions to be stable.

◦～ჟ

On Sunday, September 17th, eighty-six days after being admitted to the hospital for their tissue expansion, followed by separation surgery, the twins were released. This had been a day I'd waited for somewhat impatiently. I was tired of hospitals, but the girls never complained.

We knew it would be a long time until full recovery, but being home felt like progress.

CHAPTER 26

September 2006

Our extended family threw a "baby" shower the day before we brought the girls home so they had new clothes. I chose skirts and white shirts with sweaters for them to wear home. Jake's sister, Amy, came into the hospital to French braid their hair.

Courtney came with us that morning, too. We wanted to go home as the same family we had been when the girls were born. We held a press conference in the foyer and brought Kendra and Maliyah out for everyone to see. Afterward the media followed us home, where the real party would begin.

The twins were fussy and cried a little when they were put into car seats. Maybe they were uncomfortable or perhaps unsure what their bodies were supposed to do. This was another first of so many more that would come. Both girls had an oxygen cannula in her nose, and the portable machines made the same rhythmic soothing noise they were used to. After only a few blocks, the crying stopped.

I glanced back to see the twins smiling and taking in everything they saw. They hadn't been outside for months, so the world must have seemed new.

When we pulled up to the house, we were amazed at how many family members and friends were there to greet us. A huge "Welcome Home" sign hung from the garage, and everyone applauded when we took the girls out of the car. We let the media stay for about ten minutes of picture taking, and then I told them it was time to go.

We were stunned by how many people cared. Jake had set up a Web site to post updates about the girls after they were born, and once the news channels had started giving out the web address, we soon had over 800,000 hits. We didn't think this was the last we would see of the news crews.

Inside the house we celebrated with cake and ice cream, and the girls sat in high chairs for the first time. Afterwards, I took Kendra downstairs where she tried to play with her younger cousins, her brothers, and her sister. She was so tired she soon fell asleep.

Four weeks later, Kendra was back for additional surgery. The doctors worked with her skin, but it took another five months before her wounds were completely healed. During that time, she was taken in for regular hyperbaric chamber treatments to help with the skin re-growth where the wounds were. She loved going to see her friends there. Here she was, this four-year-old, life-of-the party girl going into the chamber with seventy-year-old men. It was amazing.

During Kendra's first treatment, they had to poke a hole in her ear drum so she could withstand the pressure of the chamber. She was so brave as they did that twice—once for each ear. I don't think I could have done it once.

I don't know if the girls were trying to gain their independence from each other or because they weren't feeling well or what, but after they were separated, they fought a lot at first.

"Mom, she's . . ." started a lot of the sentences I heard throughout the day. I tried to help them solve the problems, but words didn't always work at bringing the peace.

Of course, now we could put them in separate rooms if we needed to.

CHAPTER 27

October 2006

Because the girls were so sick and their skin tender, we added thick pads to the mattress, hoping to prevent bed sores or injury to the newly formed skin. They each had their own white twin bed, but they didn't seem to care. They wanted to sleep together, but we knew they shouldn't until their bodies had more time to heal.

Of course, the trips to the hospital weren't over. My sister-in-law, Amy, and I took them to the hospital where Kendra continued hyperbaric treatments five days a week from 7:00 a.m. to 2:00 p.m. Maliyah had dialysis for four hours from 9:00 a.m. to 1:00 p.m. They each had huge wounds on their stomach area, so three days a week we spent an additional three hours getting the VAC dressing changed. That meant I was gone for nine hours those days and my other children didn't have their mother.

Grandma Patsy was there for them, and they were good, but eventually they were frustrated with having both Mom and Dad gone from home for such long hours.

As the girls began to heal, they felt better too. They became upset when they couldn't move the way they wanted to, but soon each one learned to use a crutch. The wheelchair had been fine and crawling or pulling themselves up to pieces of furniture had been okay, even if it wasn't always the best option. But standing up and walking alone was exciting for both of the girls. They were in heaven. Jake and I started discussing the possibility of getting them each a prosthetic leg, a "helper leg" like the mother of another set of separated conjoined twins called it. Their progress gave us hope.

And like the progress with their mobility, the hope for a kidney transplant also became closer. From the beginning, the doctors had wanted to perform the transplant six to seven months after the separation surgery. All of us continued to monitor Maliyah's progress. We knew we couldn't leave her on dialysis, yet we needed a kidney for her now that the girls were separated. We worried because she was having some feeding issues. She couldn't eat most things because her body didn't know what to do with the nutrients. Eating made her literally unhealthy, so she had tube feedings and was only allowed six ounces of water a day.

I had known since the beginning that I wanted to be the kidney donor for Maliyah. The doctors told us that the donor must have a positive match for at least three of six factors in the blood and tissue types to reduce the possibility of rejection. I matched my daughter in five, so there was no need to test for other possible donors, even though we had countless numbers of people offer, including strangers.

There was a concern about my recovery, however. The doctors warned me that it might take at least six weeks for me to recover from the kidney removal surgery.

"I don't know if I can do that," I said as we discussed the possibility. "I'm basically the caretaker for the girls, and I'm the one who keeps the ball rolling."

I was worried that if anything happened to me, it would put Jake over the edge.

"We want to make sure this is best for everyone," the team of doctors agreed.

I wanted to be the one to donate, and I needed one additional test before everything was ready—a CT scan.

The machine wasn't quite as daunting as the one had been for the MRI, but I still had to pass though a tube, a shallow one this time. The girls had done this so many times now. I knew I had to do it to. It was the only way for the surgeons to see exactly where my kidneys were positioned, which one was better in size and location for them to get, and how many veins led to it.

Honestly, this CT scan was no big deal and was actually easier than the treadmill stress test to check the health of my heart. And the blood tests! I had to give them a lot of blood because they needed to test for everything under the sun. We couldn't afford for Maliyah to experience any problems.

Once all the test results were back, we knew for sure. I'd be Maliyah's donor, and we prayed the kidney would fit in the place the surgeon planned to position it within her small body.

Chapter 28

April 2007

I'm not even nervous about getting a kidney, Mom," Maliyah said the morning of the operation. She'd become an old pro at surgeries, like it or not.

I couldn't say the same. Oh, I wasn't nervous about giving her my kidney. I was nervous because they were taking me into surgery before her. I didn't want to leave my little girl alone, even for a minute.

As it turned out, I spent all that worry for nothing. She went in first after all, and she didn't even cry. I had told her getting a kidney meant no more dialysis, and that made her happy. No more spending hours each day attached to that machine. No more throwing up ten or fifteen times a day and having her eyes burn and body hurt because of the treatments. All those memories made her want this surgery even more than before.

We were scheduled for 8:00 a.m. I remember waking briefly—almost like a dream—during the operation and asking the anesthesiologist, "Is my kidney pink?" Pink was the color the kidney should be when Maliyah's blood was running through it properly.

"It is," he assured me, and I went back to sleep.

It only seemed moments had passed when I woke up over eight hours later in my room at Primary Children's. I was in a lot of pain and disoriented from the drugs, but I wanted to go see Maliyah to make sure she was okay. I couldn't though because of my own condition. Instead, Holly Moss Rosen, the Child Life Specialist, took photos of her and brought them down for me to see.

I guess my nerves weren't satisfied by photos alone because that night I had a panic attack. The doctor ended up giving me a strong sedative so I would sleep. I needed the rest if my own incision were to heal. I was twenty-six years old, and I had worked hard to keep physically fit, but recovery from surgery would be taxing to my system.

When I woke the next morning, I was worried how Maliyah's body was functioning with my kidney—her new kidney.

"Everything is fine," the nurse assured me.

"How do you know?" I asked. "Can someone prove it?"

A few minutes later, Holly gave me the proof I wanted. She came into my room and handed over a new stack of photos. "Maliyah's pee," she said.

And sure enough, there were photos of her urine-filled catheter bag. I was so touched that I cried. "No more dialysis," I said, the relief obvious in my voice. The kidney was working.

I was so happy I had kept my body strong and healthy so I could give her a second gift of life, one that would now be more normal and free. Dialysis wasn't a life and never would be; no quality of life could ever come from it for my little girl.

The challenges her body had faced without a kidney had been great enough. Dialysis offered its own challenges, more than just the amount of time it took. Of course, there had never been time off from the three days a week, no matter what. Now she wouldn't have to be tied to that schedule. And her body would become stronger because she could heal.

Even the other kids were excited when they heard the news from Grandma Patsy that Maliyah's kidney was functioning. No more dialysis meant we could go places and do more things together as a family.

But first I needed to see Maliyah and hold her. I got it stuck in my head that the medical staff wasn't taking good enough care of my baby, that they were hurting her.

"I want to see her now!" I said, despite the assurances I got from all of them, as well as Jake that Maliyah was doing great. I couldn't be reasoned with it seemed. At last I asked Jake and his brother Bruce to give her another blessing.

Jake went down to her room to meet with the two nurses assigned to monitor her constantly. A few minutes later, he came back to report that he had administered the blessing and Maliyah opened her eyes briefly at the sound of his voice.

Despite this good news, I was inconsolable until at last the medications took the edge off my pain, and I slept. When I awoke, the surgeon came to visit and told me that the transplant had been easy. I'm not a very big woman and my kidney was smaller than an average adult's, so it fit Maliyah perfectly. He also felt that the anxiety I was feeling was caused by the pain medications and that the effect was similar to the reaction Kendra and Maliyah had both had from the same medicine.

The media covered the surgery, although we thought it was only important to our family. I guess I was wrong. Maliyah and I both received Get Well cards, flowers, and small gifts from people we didn't know.

I spent another two days in the hospital. Five-year-old Maliyah was there for three weeks total, but the biggest worry was over. She had a kidney. She and Kendra were both healing, and the future looked brighter all the time for our entire family.

CHAPTER 29

December 2008

The bright future wasn't yet to be. Six weeks after the transplant, Maliyah experienced terrible pains in her abdomen, and we took her in for an evaluation. Her blood levels had changed, so they admitted her to the hospital for monitoring. We feared she was rejecting the kidney.

As the night progressed, she was in even more pain, crying out because her stomach was distended. They gave her pain medications, but it didn't seem to be enough. I was a wreck and took out my anger and fears on the doctors.

"Do something!" I shouted.

"You knew this might happen," they said as though that would calm me down.

It only made me angrier. Could they really believe this wasn't hurting me the same way it was hurting her? I hadn't recovered yet myself from the surgery, and the thought that I had given her my kidney and now her body was already trying to reject it—to push it out—was more than I could emotionally bear.

As it turned out, her body tried to reject the kidney, but we thank our Father in Heaven that it didn't succeed. New medicines were given to her; others had their levels adjusted, and the kidney rejection stopped—and hasn't returned since. It was another miracle.

Since that time we have passed many milestones and witnessed many miracles.

Kendra and Maliyah are now in school. Although their first few months were difficult for all of us, both girls love attending and are sad when they have to miss because of illness or additional surgeries.

Today, Courtney is very active in dance. She is on a competition team, and even when she isn't in class, she is dancing. She has been teaching Kendra and Maliyah some new steps at home.

Austin and Justin are very busy little boys. They just started preschool and they love Thomas the Train, playing outside with their sisters, and getting into everything.

Jake enjoys watching the kids, as well as sports when he's not actually playing them. I am pleased to report that we are still happily married.

As for me, life as a mother is busy and exhausting, but, as any mother knows, rewarding. I get along very well with my one kidney. I highly recommend donation, especially when you can give this gift of life to someone else.

As a family, we love to have movie nights and bask in the progress of our children.

Maliyah continues to be shy, yet she is such a girly-girl. When she goes to school her hair must be perfect. Yes, I said *perfect*. Kendra is outgoing and very independent, a trait that I love. Of course, she got that from me.

The girls will soon be fitted with prosthetic legs, but in the meantime, they have learned to use walkers and crutches to get around, although Maliyah prefers to scoot on the floor. They undergo daily physical therapy and there have been additional surgeries, but none so involved as those they have had before.

The girls will face more surgeries and obstacles throughout their lives, but they continue to inspire those around them with their happy smiles and strong spirits.

It's been two-and-a-half years since the girls were separated. We thank our Father in Heaven every day for the privilege of having them. They have had so many blessings and opportunities in their short lives already. We look forward to a bright and hopefully less (medically) eventful future.

Although all the attention can be overwhelming at times, we're grateful for the outpouring of love that was (and is) so important to us at the most difficult times. We know that all the prayers in our behalf brought to us the many miracles that we experienced.

Kendra and Maliyah don't see themselves as any more special than their friends at school, but at home we do. These two girls are our miracles, and they have brought us together with family, medical professionals, and friends old and new, helping us all gain a greater respect and appreciation for all the miracles in our lives.

Happiness and joy can be found in the most heart-wrenching circumstances when it brings us closer to God, family and friends. This love, combined with faith, helps us endure any trials that come our way.

Because when hearts conjoin, miracles happen.

They really do.

Blessing Day Spring 2002

Two Peas in a Pod

Twins at play

"Give Kids the World" Orlando

Courtney with Disney's Cinderella

Kendra and Maliyah in front, cousin Haley and Courtney in back

Separate but still in one wagon

Christmas 2003

Look what we can do!

The twins with cousin William

Happy together

Jeff Warren raising money for cancer research with the entire family

Courtney, Grandpa Jeff and Maliyah

Erin's favorite photo with Courtney

Christmas 2005

Family of seven with new beautiful baby boys, Justin and Austin

Angie Larsen from Good Things Utah, ABC 4, with all the Herrin children

Jake with Justin and Austin

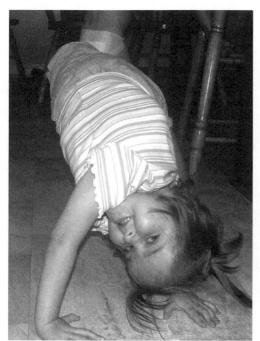

Two little monkeys

Austin, Erin and Justin swimming at Grandma and Grandpa Warren's

Beautiful girls with beautiful smiles

Our favorite family photo

Join Our Mailing List

Join the Herrin family mailing list and receive free exclusive family updates, news and information about events in your area. To join the Herrin mailing list go to:

www.herrintwins.com.

Additional Sources

———— ✑ ————

Fierro, P.P. Conjoined twins profile: Kendra and Maliyah Herrin. About.com.
http://multiples.about.com/cs/conjoinedprofiles/p/aactherrin.htm?p=1
   Retrieved September 27, 2008.

Free, C. Conjoined twins find life apart. Reader's Digest. September 2008.
www.rd.com
   Retrieved December 20, 2008.

Herrin, Jake. (2003-2009) Herrin Twins
www.HerrinTwins.com
   Retrieved January 19, 2009.

The Associated Press. Conjoined Twins, 4, to be separated.
MSNBC.com. August 4, 2006.
www.msnbc.msn.com/id/14170936
   Retrieved September 27, 2008.

Wikipedia: Kendra and Maliyah Herrin
http://En.wikipedia,org/wiki/Kendra_and_Maliyah_Herrin.27
   Retrieved September 27, 2008.

About the Authors

— Q —

E RIN MARIE HERRIN is first and foremost a mother. She loves playing with her five children, scrapbooking, traveling, and playing jokes on her family. Thrust into the spotlight after the birth of Kendra and Maliyah, the Herrin story has been featured on Good Morning America, 20/20, the Today Show, The Glenn Beck show, Inside Edition, Access Hollywood, Fox News, MSNBC News and written up in hundreds of newspapers and magazines worldwide including *People, In Touch*, and *Reader's Digest*. Erin has also been a regular guest on the Oprah Winfrey show. The Herrin family is currently filming a special for the TLC network. Erin is available for speaking engagements and can be reached at herrinfamily@herrintwins.com.

Lu Ann Brobst Staheli, M.Ed., is an accomplished educator and writer. She has the honor of being Utah's 2008 Best of State Educator K-12, Utah English Language Arts Teacher of the Year, Nebo Reading Teacher of the Year, Utah Valley League of Utah Writers Writer of the Year, Utah Arts Council Juvenile Novel  Author of the Year, League of Utah Writers Diamond Quill and Juvenile Novel Author of the Year, and Christa McAuliffe Fellow. Lu Ann teaches English at Payson Junior High in addition to being a writer. She resides in Spanish Fork, Utah, with her husband and five sons. Lu Ann is available for speaking engagements and may be reached at: luannbrobststaheli@gmail.com.